HUMANISTIC JUDAISM

Sherwin T. Wine

Prometheus Books
Buffalo, New York 14215

Published by Prometheus Books
1203 Kensington Avenue, Buffalo, New York 14215

Library of Congress Catalog Card Number 77-90496
ISBN 0-87975-102-9

Printed in the United States of America

CONTENTS

iii

FOREWORD

Hillel was once asked to summarize Judaism while his questioner stood on one foot. Without responding in anger to what seemed colossal *hutspa*, he replied: "What is hateful to yourself do not do to your neighbor. That is the Torah. All the rest is commentary."

The answer is famous. But, of course, quite unsatisfactory. Not that the reply is ethically reprehensible, but that it is the ultimate moral cliché. It is just too universal and too presumptuous. To identify the uniqueness of Judaism with the golden rule is to imply a Jewish monopoly on compassion. Certainly Hillel's statement doesn't distinguish Judaism from either Christianity or Confucianism. It simply articulates what *all* civilized religions subscribe to.

Despite the inadequacy of his answer, I am intrigued by Hillel's problem. Many people (prompted more by a genuine interest than by *hutspa*) approach me asking for instant summaries of the basic principles of Humanistic Judaism. Although I am not much given to writing missionary tracts, a sense of the inadequacy of any "instant summary" has led me to attempt in this collection of essays to state the unique combination of ideas that define the religious approach of the Society for Humanistic Judaism.

My hope is that this book will articulate the thoughts and feelings of many Jews who wish to remain Jews but who find themselves uncomfortable with the official ideology of the Jewish establishment.

Without the careful assistance of many people, Robert Barr and Miriam Jerris in particular, this book would not have been possible.

Sherwin T. Wine

I
INTRODUCTION

The most interesting Jews of the last one hundred years never joined a synagogue.

They never prayed.

They were disinterested in God.

They paid no attention to the Torah lifestyle.

They found bourgeois Reform as parochial as traditional Orthodoxy.

They preferred writing new books to worrying about the meaning of old books.

They had names like Albert Einstein, Sigmund Freud, and Theodore Herzl.

They were the stars of the contemporary Jewish world. No rabbi or theologian had their power or relevance.

Although they were not aware of the label, they represented the boldness and excitement of a new kind of Judaism. They were the non-deliberate prophets of Humanistic Judaism.

Humanistic Judaism is less well known than Orthodoxy, Conservatism, and Reform. But, on a behavioral level, it represents many more American Jews than any of these official ideologies.

Humanistic Judaism is the philosophy of life which motivates the actions of the vast majority of contemporary

That is why Corliss supports him

Jewry. Most humanistic Jews do not know that they are
what they are. They have never confronted their behavior.
They have never bothered to articulate the real beliefs that
lie behind their lifestyle—because, to do so, would force
them to deal with the discrepancy between what they say
they believe and what they actually do believe.

OK, but…

Perhaps you are a humanistic Jew and do not know it.

This book may help you discover your true Jewish
identity.

*→ just by reducing
it to their Jew complex?*

yes

II
REALITY *What is*

The Return to Tradition

Are Jews returning to tradition? Is orthodoxy on the upswing? Is humanism passé? Some say *yes*. They cite the following evidence.

The Lubavitcher Hasidim are popular, militant, and growing in number. The public display of the yarmulka is increasing. Reform Temples have embraced Hebrew, Bar-mitsvahs, and prayer shawls. Parochial schools are getting bigger and bigger. Rabbinic students at the Conservative Jewish Theological Seminary are doing more and more ritual. Denunciations of intermarriage are getting louder and louder. More and more Jews are wearing mezuzahs around their necks. More and more Jewish students have signed up for courses about Jewish tradition at secular universities throughout America.

What does it all mean? Have secularized Jews seen the theological light? Has the recession exposed the futility of material pursuits and revived an interest in old-time spiritual values? Have young Jews discovered that the new American lifestyle is vacuous and do they now yearn for the meaningful discipline of the old *halakha?*

Before we answer the questions, a few facts are appropriate.

Fact

1. There is no evidence that the *behavior* of Jews outside the synagogue has changed. Pre-marital sex, frequent divorce, intermarriage, and female equality are on the increase. The pursuit of leisure, pleasure, and individual happiness is absorbing not only the young but also the middle-aged and the old. The lifestyles of most contemporary Jews, even those who profess a love of tradition, are in total opposition to the decrees of both the Bible and the Talmud. A nude bathing pre-medical student who lives with her boyfriend and refuses to eat pork as an affirmation of her Jewish identity is hardly a return to tradition. Even without pork she would give Hillel a heart attack.

2. Orthodox Judaism has become Americanized. At one time the leadership of traditional Jewry was foreign and Yiddish speaking. It was unable to compete with the assimilated graces of Reform rabbis. It lacked the skills for successful social exposure. This past reality is not the present one. What we are now experiencing is the new-found articulation of people who could never before claim the public forum. Orthodox Jews today are as well-educated and Americanized as their liberal opposition. Their new-found aggressiveness is a sign of their new security in the American environment. It is not a sign that they are holding or recruiting large numbers of American Jews to traditional life. Christian fundamentalism is more vocal and more conspicuous in urban America—not because more and more people have accepted Christian piety, but especially because the lower-class Appalachian refugee has now come into his own power and affluence in Northern cities.

3. Jewish ethnicity has lost its major expression in America. The Yiddish language is, for all practical purposes, dead. A non-observant, Yiddish speaking atheist had no trouble identifying himself as a Jew or being identified as a Jew. But secularized Jews who have lost their linguistic uniqueness are now struggling to find other unique forms of Jewish behavior. In the absence of secular Jewish creativity, they are forced to turn to the one remaining behavior pattern which is uniquely Jewish—traditional

religious ritual. Since they have no serious intent to adopt a traditional lifestyle, and since they are totally divorced from the cultural context in which these rituals had meaning, they dabble in Jewish exotica. Mezuzahs which are intended for door-posts are hung around necks. Avoiding pork becomes a dramatic gesture in Chinese restaurants with tasty seafood. The kiddush becomes the family introduction to the busiest day of the week. Nostalgia in bad taste is hardly a return to tradition. It is simply a sign of secular laziness.

Is there a return to orthodoxy? Not really. In an age where lifestyles are in a constant state of flux, Jews who want to be Jewish are looking for unique ways to identify themselves to others. Nostalgia most likely will not work for long; the only solution is to create *new* Jewish rituals that really fit our *new* lifestyle.

→ what does he really mean by Jewish?

Honesty

The first need of American Jewry is *not* survival; it is honesty. Before we can plan what we should be, we have to know what we are. Before we can discuss the conditions of group endurance, we have to confront the reality that endures. Pious statements of non-existent belief will do us no good. It is ludicrous to praise bibles we do not read and gods we do not worship. It is futile to announce commitments we have long since abandoned and attachments we have clearly discarded. Self-deception is a common human art, which finds its most comfortable home in modern religious institutions.

that's what ACJ was doing

Most definitions of contemporary Judaism are the product of academic fantasies. Scholars and clergymen imagine what they *would like* Jews to believe and they proceed to equate that desire with what Jews *do* believe. There are countless books available for popular reading which propose to reveal the commitments of modern Jewry. Waxing eloquent on matters theological, their authors discuss the deep God devotion and intense worship practices of the American Jewish community. The naïve Gentile reader would assume that his local Jews were "chips off the Old Testament," pious Bible lovers who can hardly wait for their next installment of Midrashic commentary. Long discourses on the covenant between God and Israel are followed by impassioned references to the centrality of Torah in Jewish life. Modern Jewry turns out to be only an adjusted extension of good old Hillel and Akiba. Having carefully studied these documents of illusions, the realistic observer can only ask, "If there are so many Jews like the ones described, where are they?"

But the illusion is understandable. It is difficult for most people to confront what they really are and what they really believe. There are many factors, psychic and social, which inhibit our insight and prevent us from seeing the obvious. If intellectual integrity were the only human need, honesty would be easy.

In fact, we tend to determine what we believe by what we say rather than by what we do. Having certain ritual phrases of belief imprinted on our minds from childhood, we repeat them endlessly as a convenient way of describing what we have never bothered to investigate. Too often so-called sociological surveys of Jewish belief depend on the direct questioning of individuals who lack any form of self-insight. The people interviewed parrot back phrases learned in Sunday School which bear absolutely no relationship to their behavior. After all, what a man is truly committed to, he is willing to act on. If a person claims to love prayer but rarely prays, if an individual lauds the meaningfulness of God but never invokes God for the solution of his daily problems, if a man describes the Torah as the greatest of all possible books but never reads it; he is either lying or self-deceived. For what a man does is the only adequate test of a man's belief.

The pressure of society is another factor that inhibits honesty. We live in a culture where theological belief is respectable. In modern suburbia, belonging to a church or

He misuses the high energy/fervor the idolatrous and particularly the mystical belief ... pathological ... Jews that "god" will ...

synagogue and sending the children to Sunday School are more than fashionable; they are social requirements. Affiliation with a religious institution never has to be justified; non-affiliation always has to be explained. As long as one is willing to say that he believes in God (in some way or other), he is socially safe and free from the pain caused by disapproving neighbors. For Jews, who are a vulnerable ethnic minority addicted to rapid social climbing and who bear the neurotic scars of two thousand years of relentless persecution, caution is preferable to honesty. After fear has dictated our conformity, we rationalize our action by imagining that we believe what our behavior denies.

And then there is guilt. No cause of self-deception is more powerful. Since our religion is inextricably bound up with the family into which we were born, we cannot easily separate our religious practices from our family loyalties. To attempt to make this distinction is to expose ourselves to the painful disapproval of those we love. Intellectual honesty appears, in the moment of stress, a trivial obstacle to parental pressure. The challenge need not be overt. We have only to imagine the pleading faces of our venerable ancestors, who sacrificed their lives to defend what we no longer believe. It is psychically necessary for many to think that what they are saying and doing meets the expectations of their forefathers. The desperate attempt of the Reform movement to demonstrate some vital connection between its modern rationalism and the fanatic temperament of the ancient prophets is a case in point. Only guilt would have the power to drive men to such an absurd endeavor.

In order to understand the realities of what we believe, we have to pay serious attention to what we do or do not do. We have to observe what *really* excites Jews as opposed to what they *say* excites them. In other words, sociologists can give us better insight into the nature of Judaism than theologians. For example, although the synagogue is often hailed as the Jewish house of learning, it can more accurately be described in America as a permanent shelter for puberty rites. Without Barmitsvah and Confirmation its school system would lose its very reason for existence, and the temple would be abandoned to the dreary function of remembering the dead. Not that Jews have given up learning. In fact, Jews today constitute a major part of our domestic intellectual elite. They are even accused of controlling American letters and exercising massive control over academic studies. If they are better educated than ever before, it is hardly because of the synagogue. The secular university has become the new shrine for Jewish studies. Its disciplines of psychology, sociology, medicine, and law have long ago replaced the study of the Bible and rendered Talmud learning exotic even for Jews. If an objective observer desires to understand the motivating beliefs of the overwhelming majority of Jews under forty, he should devote his time to analyzing the fundamental principles of scientific and university inquiry. An intimate reading of Rabbi Akiba will do him no good. It may, at best, turn out to be a delightful exploration of what Jews used to believe.

Modern Judaism has much more to do with the methods of the secular university than with the techniques of the Talmudic rabbis. Empiricism, pragmatism, and free inquiry are far more characteristic of the truth seeking procedures of contemporary Jews than attachment to prophetic revelation. One may approve or deplore this situation, but neither sentiment will reverse the change. One may summon all Jews back from their "sinful heresies," denounce their disloyalty, invoke the suffering faces of their ancient martyrs, and bemoan the changes with tired contempt. But the new reality will not be altered. An ironic transformation has come to pass: Orthodoxy, by virtue of the secular revolution, has ceased to be Jewish. Like the Sabbath day in America, it is something for Seventh Day Adventists—and not for Jews.

Nor will the Bible game survive much scrutiny. Reform rabbis may arrange countless interfaith banquets where the Torah devotion of their congregants is announced and applauded. They may do dramatic readings of the psalms and clever reinterpretations of Bible verses. They may even expose the world to the unknown Talmudic wonders of Jewish history. But to no avail. An objective survey of present Jewish reading reveals that most Jews rarely open the Bible and never study the Talmud. Despite the nostalgic novels of Potok, Agnon, and Singer, the Jews have found new and more exciting study materials. After they have paid their customary tribute to the glories of ancient Jewish literature, they read something else.

As for the life of prayer and worship, it exists as a very dim memory in the psyche of the suburban Jew. While it is periodically indulged at Barmitsvahs and Yahrzeits, it is a somewhat vicarious experience, in which the rabbi, cantor, or choir perform for a passive audience. The reason for this laxity is clear. To the skeptical, analytic, and sophisticated mind, worship is difficult; and to the devotee who has redefined God as a natural impersonal force, prayer is silly. Without the imagined presence of an awesome, all-powerful father figure the whole structure of Jewish worship collapses. The recent Reform revision of the Union Prayer Book seems a bit anachronistic. Why bother to improve prayers for people who don't want to pray? Perhaps more drastic alternatives are needed.

If one objectively surveys the Jewish activity of adult Jews in an American metropolitan community, he immediately notices that most of this activity has nothing whatever to do with what is usually called religious practice. Aside from ghetto socializing, the only uniquely Jewish cause which excites Jews is uninvolved with either theology or worship. This cause is the state of Israel. The June war revealed to many blasé sophisticates the reality of their Jewish involvement. Their excitement sometimes puzzled and disturbed them—but it was real and could not be denied. The Israeli attachment is the very reverse of the theological commitment. In America we tend, for reasons of social safety, to overstate the genuineness of a theological conviction we have gradually abandoned and to understate the depth of an ethnic attachment our behavior clearly reveals.

The reality of what Jews actually do is the best evidence of the character of modern Judaism. Existing Jewish practice gives no indication that there persists in the American community the kind of religious conviction that motivates people to live by the classic standards of either the Bible or the Talmud. Contemporary Jewish culture is university oriented and scientifically indoctrinated. Present day middle class Jews have found ways other than theology to deal with their anxieties. The rabbis may cleverly poke fun at the reigning psychiatrist, but they still have to come up with a more effective alternative. Preferring Moses to Freud is irrelevant in an environment where nobody reads Moses.

An honest Judaism does not describe what Jews *used* to believe; it clarifies and articulates what Jews *do* believe. Since Jewish identity is defined by society (and even by Orthodoxy) as an ethnic identity, Judaism changes from century to century. In Solomon's day it was polytheistic; in Hillel's day it was monotheistic; in our time it has, by any behavior standard, become humanistic. As long as a Jewish people persists, whatever beliefs the overwhelming majority of that people subscribes to is justifiably called Judaism. Our task is, therefore, to discard pretense, to observe our actions, and to discover what we truly believe. Without honest self-insight, we are condemned to the futile task of improving illusions.

The New Jew

The Jews of the twentieth century have become a secular people.

The Judaism of the twentieth century has become a secular 'religion.'

The deep theological convictions of historic Judaism survive as the ritual vocabulary of prayer. But they no longer carry conviction. The secular revolution which undermined Christianity and which created our contemporary urban lifestyle destroyed the Jewish God.

Urban people find very little need for God.

In an urban environment people worry about human power. The power to make weapons, the power to create pollution, the power to fly from one place to another, the power to conquer disease, the power to manufacture the necessities of life are *human* abilities. Both the good and the evil of our city setting are the creation of man. In an age when collective man felt helpless to do either in a grand style both God and the Devil were more interesting. Today *we* can do what, it was believed, they alone could do.

In an urban environment people have to rely upon themselves for moral authority. There are too many competing voices which claim to be the mouth of God. In a rural setting where *one* church and *one* synagogue authority dominated the scene, the voice of God was clear. In an urban milieu 'the word of the Lord' is confused. The ethnic melting pot features a wide variety of denominations and cults—each claiming to possess the truth. In the end, the individual, confronted with this overwhelming variety, is forced to assume the responsibility of choosing. He must choose the *real* voice. God becomes like every other item in the consumer culture; he is selected from among his competitors. It is a demeaning come down for a so-called Supreme Being.

The city environment subverts old authority. The culture of science and technology is future-oriented. It assumes that people in the future will know more than they did in the past and that old literature is less valuable than new literature. If knowledge is cumulative, if it is derived from human experience and experimental testing, the more experience and the more testing the more knowledge. The present no longer worships the wisdom of the past. It revises it on the basis of new evidence. In an urban setting of continual change the wisdom of the past becomes increasingly less relevant. It is revised right out of existence.

The modern Jew is a non-theological secular Jew. On a

behavioral level he bears no resemblance to Hillel and Akiba.

The modern Jew is an urban Jew. On the level of visible activity his lifestyle is radically different from that of Moses and David, the Baal Shem Tov and the Gaon of Vilna.

The problem of the modern Jew is not that he has changed (the change is irreversible), but that he refuses to accept the change. He feels guilty and believes that his ancestors despise him. Unable to live with this imagined disapproval, he develops cults of nostalgia and accommodation. He pretends that his lifestyle has some vital connection with the Torah and rabbinic Judaism. He designs temples which dramatize this connection and hires clergymen who demonstrate it.

Conservative and Reform Judaism are expressions of this pretending. In their passionate need for historical respectability, they are forced to distort Jewish history. To imagine that there is some essential connection between the Biblical prophets, who were pastoral fundamentalists, and the contemporary liberal urbanized Jew is an act of historical blindness. Only a desperate need to be *kosherized* by the past could have prompted it.

A free, intelligent, and good-humored approach *to* Jewish history would not allow the past to tyrannize over the present. This approach would include self-esteem that would obviate the need for a *kosherized* history. This approach would make the present, most likely, a lot more interesting than the Jewish past—that the modern, urban cosmopolitan Jew is a lot more significant than his Biblical, hill-country predecessor.

Instead of apologizing to the past for having abandoned what was worthy of being abandoned, the Jew of dignity takes pride in contemporary Jewish sophistication and power. Instead of feeling guilty about not believing in God, he feels relieved.

Instead of feeling shame in rejecting the lifestyle of Maimonides, he feels fortunate in being able to do what

Maimonides, hemmed in by the hateful pressures of social opinion, could not do.

Instead of experiencing regret in rarely reading the Bible or the Talmud, he takes pleasure in the fact that there were so many exciting secular Jewish poets, dramatists, novelists, and philosophers who truly inspire him and make sense.

The Jew of dignity simply stops defending himself before the past. He affirms the value of the present.

The French Revolution, the Enlightenment, and the open society have been good for the Jews. By liberating them for full participation in the life of a universal urban culture, they enabled them to fully develop the intellectual abilities which their bourgeois background had suppressed or redirected into the useless games of Talmudic *pilpul.*

A religion which was appropriate to hill-country priests in 500 B.C., or to prosperous merchants in agricultural Spain, or to destitute craftsmen in peasant Poland is simply inappropriate to the citizens of megalopolis. No legal fictions, no textual twisting can ultimately hide that reality.

Can we accept what we are without self-hate?

The conventional commentators are wrong. Disliking the lifestyle of the Jewish past is *not* self-hate. Pretending to love it—when one has already chosen to live another—*is* an act of self-hate.

Who are my ancestors that they alone should be my judges? I can like myself only when I can, in turn, accept them as my defendants.

The Jew of dignity knows how to deal effectively with the antisemite.

The modern antisemite does not hate the Jew because 'he killed Christ'. Raised in a secular society, he has long since given up any sincere attachment to Christian ideology.

The modern antisemite, from Drumont to Chamberlain to Hitler, hates the Jew because he is the best adapted of modern peoples to life in urban civilization. Two thousand years of bourgeois experience have given the Jews city skills that even the burdensome Torah could not negate.

The *new* antisemite is ambivalent. In transition from his agricultural past to his urban future, he is unsure of himself and what he is. Divorced from the old religion, which is no longer meaningful, and searching for a new religion, which will give structure to his new experience of mobility, isolation, and family breakdown, he lashes out at the most visible symbol of *urban* success—the ultimate city-slicker—the Jew.

In the literature of contemporary antisemitism, the Jew is the symbol of everything about the city culture which defines its character and which the fearful novice finds threatening: Mobility, Intellectuality, Science, Skepticism, Innovation, Money, Atheism, and Aggressiveness.

The Jewish response to antisemitism has been without dignity. It has been a response of self-hate. Instead of accepting with good humor and the pleasure of success the fact that we are essentially mobile, intellectual, science-oriented, skeptical, innovative, money-expert, behaviorally atheistic, and creatively pushy, we cringe with the disgust of self-awareness and then proceed to deny what we are.

We create the Reform movement and pretend that we have become the eternal witnesses to God and the Bible.

We invent the Conservative movement and play synagogue games where we dress up like our pre-Enlightenment ancestors.

We embrace Zionism and prove to the world that Jews can be farmers like everybody else and that they have the same love of soil and land that Germans and Russians have.

Zionism is the ultimate expression of—not the answer to—Jewish self-hate. Instead of confronting the antisemite and telling him that the Jews enjoyed what the antisemite feared and that someday he too would be doing what Jews are doing with pleasure, the Zionist accepted the value system of his accuser. There *was* something wrong in not working with one's own hands. There *was* something wrong in not living close to the soil. There *was* something wrong in being cosmopolitan and in not having a language that one could call one's own.

Zionism was an attempt to repudiate the urban lifestyle of the modern Jew, which has fortunately transcended the mystique of sacred real estate. It was an attempt to affirm the value of the pre-urban ethics of the antisemite and to reawaken that romantic nostalgia in Jews. The Jew was to destroy in himself what the antisemite could not stand.

In the end, Zionism lost. The state of Israel, like every other modern nation, is the 'victim' of relentless, universal urban culture. They do the same things in Tel Aviv that they do in Miami and London. The consumer culture is transnational. Detroit—and the automobile civilization it founded—has done a lot more to mold modern Jerusalem than modern Jerusalem has done to mold Detroit.

Humanistic Judaism is a reponse to the secular revolution, which allows the modern Jew to do what Reform, Conservativism, and Zionism did not allow him to do—accept himself as he *is* not as he *was.* ? Ambivalent!

Humanistic Judaism starts with the affirmation that the *new* Jew—the mobile, the intellectual, the science-oriented, the skeptical, the innovative, the money-expert, the atheistic, and aggressive Jew—is *real* and *ok*. In fact, he is more interesting and more significant to world culture than any Jew who preceded him.

The University Religion

The survival of Jewish identity in the American diaspora is a function of the new social status which Jews have achieved. Secure in their New-World environment, Jews can now indulge the contemporary religious dilemma without the accusations of racial treason and cowardly desertion. When being Jewish is becoming vaguely fashionable, ceasing to be Jewish is hardly dishonorable.

The old forces that promoted Jewish identification through organized affiliation are quickly dissipating and leaving the option of easy non-involvement. While antisemitism fluctuates with the economic cycle, alternative scapegoats and the breakdown of traditional social patterns have rendered it less important. And while family pressures with all their attendant guilt feelings still give a strong push to conformity and synagogue involvement, a highly mobile society is freeing thousands of Jews from the immediate presence of parental demands. After the last "Bobe" and "Zayde" dies and conventional guilt-twisting becomes less painful, the Barmitsvah bandwagon that sustains the modern synagogue may grind to a halt. And if the synagogue goes, the one remaining barrier between organized Jewish identity and none at all will have fallen. As with German-Americans, only the last names will linger on as linguistic relics of a bygone attachment.

To appeal to Jewish loyalty on the basis of the contemporary doctrines of Orthodoxy, Conservatism, and Reform, is to indulge fantasy. In a nation where over eighty percent of Jewish youth attend secular colleges and universities, the belief framework of any conventional Judaism is irrelevant to the intellectual forces and authority figures that are molding the Jewish mind. The grandfathers of contemporary Jewry had a wider basis of communication with as distant a figure as Rabbi Akiba than they had with their own grandchildren. It is a rather obvious fact that most young Jews today simply do not believe, in any vital way, what their ancestors believed.

Their world outlook is much more attuned to Bertrand Russell than to Jeremiah. Clever clergymen may try through labored exegesis to demonstrate that there is no real conflict between the "mainstream" of Judaism and the premises of modern science, but their attempts do no credit to either historic Judaism or to modern science.

If Judaism is to find a future in America, it must transcend clichéd appeals to group loyalty and deal realistically with the beliefs that motivate Jewish behavior.

The dominant ideology of the American Jewish situation is what may be designated as "the university religion."

Although most young Jews are not consciously aware of its premises or would not be able to articulate its principles, it is the truth procedure that pervades secular educational institutions. Few people exposed to the environment of the American public school and college can escape its influence, if not its conquest.

There are three fundamentals to the "university religion," which influence our contemporary culture and which stand in contrast to the mood and method of traditional Judaism: (1) free inquiry, (2) empiricism, and (3) humanism. Let us briefly explore each of these bases.

1. Free inquiry. It is more than obvious that neither Judaism, nor any other historic religion, was committed to the principle of limitless challenges. The notion that no idea or value is free from the option of rejection denies the possibility of sacredness. Holiness is built around the feelings of "taboo" and "untouchability." Whatever is sacred evokes the appropriate response of reverence and worship; it cannot tolerate conditional acceptance, detailed measurement, or critical humor. Free inquiry would demand that the gods, if they be around, must subject themselves to psychological testing and personality evaluation. Even the most familiar moral values cannot escape the status of profanity. If investigation knows no bounds then nothing can be sacred or worshipable. The strongest commitment one can achieve is conditional respect.

In the secular age it is impossible to speak of the "sancta" of religion. A consistent naturalism denounces the sacred as an invitation to idolatry. Empirical prudishness simply resurrects a new "supernatural."

2. Empiricism. Free inquiry without responsibility is manifestly harmful. In the secular age the procedure of intuitive faith is irresponsible since it provides no method for the resolution of intuition conflicts. Empirical procedures seem best able to achieve for us what we ordinarily mean by 'truth'. They also provide through the evidence of controlled investigation a public way to resolve conflicts. They therefore make discussion possible.

Empiricism forbids what historic Judaism allowed: (1) eternal answers which subsequent experience can never refute; and (2) the verification of a statement through the discovery of its author. The second allowance involves the traditional belief that if one can demonstrate that Moses, Isaiah, Jeremiah, or some other authority figure uttered a certain informational statement, the statement is true. For the empiricist, however, the author is irrelevant; the experiential consequences are what count.

Moreover, the consistent empiricist refuses to regard as meaningful "answers" about man and the universe that make no experiential difference. Most theological assertions achieve this status. While the God of the fundamentalist may be an illusion, he at least purports to be "real" in the world of space-time. The God of the liberal theologian is so divorced from the test of empirical criteria that the same evidence can demonstrate his existence as well as his nonexistence. Believing in "ultimate reality," "necessary existence," the "ground of being," or "a power that makes for good" is derived from the same empirical base as nonbelieving.

A statement that has no possible refutation is meaningless as an affirmation. Like the emperor's clothes in Andersen's Fairy Tales, its sole reality is in the words.

3. Humanism. The author of value is man himself. "Good" and "bad" are functions of human need and desire; and intrinsic values do not stand in lonely independence. Information about the universe can help man achieve his ultimate values; it can never give them to him. To discover a "direction" in the universe is never comforting until one evaluates the tendency. Even if the gods were empirically real, obedience to them would depend on whether the individual viewed the obedience helpful or harmful, good or bad, valuable or evil. The idea of the individual as an end in himself breeds autonomy.

Traditional theism and historic Western religion stand in contrast to this view. The author of value is God, from whom man is not separable, as the child is not separable

from his father. Through an obvious psychological association, the celestial father-figure is alone considered important enough to be the creator of value.

If religion, in the broadest sense, is regarded as a search
for "meaning," that is, a search for what is intrinsically
valuable, then humanism is such a religion. While humanism accepts the fact that statements of extrinsic value,
information statements aimed at achieving finite values,
are objective and empirically responsible, it recognizes that
intrinsic value is relative and subjective, and a function of
personal intuition. Ultimate values are neither universal
nor permanent.

Humanism, empiricism, and free inquiry are the dominant principles and mood of the university world which is
presently molding the Jewish mind. They do not have to
come to terms with Judaism; it is rather Judaism that has
to come to terms with them. It may have a chance of doing
so if the following steps are taken by the progressive Jewish
religious leadership.

1. Judaism must be affirmed as a cultural and aesthetic
framework in which a variety of philosophic outlooks are
possible. Both mystic theism and empirical humanism
should feel equally at home. Jewish custom and ceremony
are an adjustable poetry, capable of embracing a wide
spectrum of human values and experiences.

2. Jewish religious activity must be "dereligionized,"
that is, secularized. There can be no idea, word, value, or
ritual that is a *sanctum,* an untouchable item of reverence.
Even Jewish survival must be periodically reviewed, with
the option of rejection as perfectly respectable.

3. Empiricism must be acknowledged as the only reliable
way to informational truth. Intuitive faith as the final
plunge to deal with questions of origin and destiny for
which there are no empirical answers is intolerable. Uncertainty is not the sign of a bad religion; it is the mark of a
wise one.

Of course the empirical method renders the old Jewish
texts intellectually dispensable. If the truths they contain

are discoverable through independent research, their usefulness is purely historical and aesthetic.

4. The language of religion must be meaningful; "God"-
language is beyond redemption. Its history is irrevocably
tied up with the person of a celestial father-figure and
cannot be divorced from the association. Moreover, sophisticated theology, in its desperate attempt to escape this embarrassing belief, has compounded the difficulty by render-
ing "God" empirically irrelevant.

Many humanists need religious services in which they
can express their shared value commitments in the context
of a community. But "God"-language, no matter how
freshly interpreted, can never create a humanistic setting,
because language communicates ideas, not only feelings.
The vocabulary of belief must be as direct as possible.

5. Jewish religious societies should be organized to
provide a sense of community support for Jewish humanists. They should bring people together who share certain
basic intrinsic values. One group may prefer to build its
program around social compassion, another around intellectual discovery, another around "mystic" peak experiences. In every case they would choose to use a demythol-
ogized Jewish aesthetics to tie the group together.

6. Jewish religious leaders must accept the "painful"
truth that for the modern American-Jewish humanist,
steeped in the milieu of an English-speaking culture,
Jewishness is a secondary value. It is an aesthetic option
which his situation both imposes on him and enables him
to appreciate. The failure of so many Jewish-survival
discussions to achieve any viable or realistic program is
derived from the illusion that Judaism in America can re-
achieve a primary significance. The Jewish philosophic
guide must, first of all, be a sensitive empiricist, interested
in the individuality of each of his students. His second task
is Jewish involvement. Ironically, the key to Jewish
survival is to adjust to this reality.

III

AVOIDING REALITY

Theology

The crisis of religion today is a crisis of belief. In a scientific age when the empirical method dominates the pursuit of truth, the belief frameworks that sustained conventional religious activity have collapsed. What a man believes about himself and his universe determines how he behaves, and, therefore, a change in belief is no trivial matter.

The decline of prayer and worship among thousands of the educated middle class (who, unlike the urban proletariat, have no economic ax to grind with church hierarchy) is a direct consequence of altered belief. No man can be motivated to pray when he has lost the possibility of a personal God; and no individual can be persuaded to worship when he views all persons, objects, feelings, and forces as ideal items for analysis and measurement. If, indeed, religion is dependent on the notions of a personal deity and sacred mystery, then it will be sustained in twentieth-century America not by individual conviction, but by social inertia.

In our contemporary culture the institutions that most effectively "imitate" the historic functions of organized religion are no longer the churches and synagogues. In the areas of pageantry, pilgrimage, and wisdom prestige, the secular schools and universities have become our modern shrines. While the clergy of urban America are peripheral powers (whose weakness is hidden by immense respectability), the academic leadership in the social, physical, and biological sciences has become the new priesthood (whose strength is disguised by the novelty of power). Much of the social reverence that used to be directed toward priestly hierarchies and church establishments is now directed toward academic institutions. The major reason for this significant shift of respect is the new belief that the university, and not the church, is the source of extraordinary power in our present society.

In fact, the issue of "extraordinary power" is the issue of religion; for all historic religions have been structured attempts to deal with those powers and forces that contemporary wisdom viewed as significant. Persons or things, celestial or earthly, possessing an immense potential to implement or frustrate human happiness and survival, have always been of religious interest. The emotions of adoration and awesome fear are normal human reactions to confrontation with great power. Gods are not religiously interesting because they are gods; they are religiously interesting because they are powerful. Both the Epicureans and the primitive Buddhists believed in the existence of gods; and both found divinities religiously irrelevant, since the deities they believed in were helpless to influence human salvation.

Modern man is still concerned with the age-old religious question: "How do I discover and use the extraordinary powers of my universe in order to achieve my happiness?" The programs of salvation, outlined by Jews, Christians, Moslems, Buddhists, Confucianists, and hosts of other groups normally identified as religious, are all related to this question. It is false to assert that historic religion has been God-centered in terms of goal; it has always been man-centered and a function of human need and desire, for how else would you motivate man to follow the program? From the point of view of most historic religions, God is a means to an end. He is overwhelmingly significant not because he is God, but because, it is believed, his power and presence are indispensable to human happiness. If, on the contrary, one believes that God is powerless to influence human welfare, he is justifiably ignored as religiously irrelevant.

Moreover, the meaninglessness of life does not arise out of man's lack of purpose or goal. All men consciously desire happiness (a favorable balance of satisfaction over frustration). The meaninglessness of life arises out of the belief that in this universe happiness is not achievable, that man's "destiny" is frustration. Religion has historically been identified with the quest for meaning, not because it has provided man with the goal of life, but because it has affirmed that the established goal was achievable and outlined the procedures necessary for such achievement.

A viable modern religion must enable man to understand and use the significant forces within and without him that make life meaningful. The decline of traditional religion is due to the ever-increasing belief that the old religion is unrelated to the social and physical forces that count. An effective contemporary viewpoint must acknowledge this problem and must clearly direct human attention to those forces that *do* count. A useful religion is always open to new information and revises its hierarchy of significant powers on the basis of new evidence.

Under these circumstances, it is obvious that theology, as a source of information about available powers, is an anachronism. In the middle ages theology was the "queen of the sciences"; no other discipline was more important. It was universally believed that without proper knowledge of God's desire and God's power human salvation was not possible. Therefore, any disclosure about God was crucial. To ignore theology would be to ignore happiness; it would be a deliberate act of masochism.

But the modern world has effected a dramatic change. The contemporary university, the center of wisdom authority, is devoid of theological interest. Hosts of students pass through its discipline, vitally absorbed with the powers that influence and control their destiny, and yet with total indifference to the issue of God. Theology has become an academic irrelevance. In the practical religion of faculty and students, God has ceased to be a significant power and is, therefore, "religiously" uninteresting. He survives in most intellectual circles as a nostalgic word and as a nod to social respectability.

The "death" of theology is not something to be deplored; it was inevitable in an age which applauds the procedures of science. What is deplorable is the inability of organized religion to dispense with a study which inhibits its religious effectiveness. The repeated theological furors of the postwar years are no sign of renewed vitality; they are the noisy friction between religious vested interests and the university culture which resists them.

There are four good reasons why theology stands in the way of an effective religion.

1. Religion should be identified with the most effective procedure for the achievement of informational truth available today. That procedure is the empirical or scientific method. The virture of this method is that it is responsible to the structured evidence of public experience and not to the whim of personal feeling and intuition. Its additional virtue is that it is self-correcting. Since truth is a product of the evidence of sense-experience, and new experience is always forthcoming, there can be no fixed statements about the world. How man views the power structure of the universe is continually alterable. Specific conclusions can be revised without the necessity of rejecting the method that sponsored them.

While Biblical theology relied on a naïve empiricism, citing unusual events, voices, apparitions, and personal conversations with God as evidence for divine reality, the classical theology that emerged in the middle ages denied the relevance of sense-experience to the demonstration of theological truth. Since God was metaphysical (beyond space-time), observable events in space-time could neither demonstrate nor refute the nature or power of God. Personal intuition and inner certainty became the sophisticated alternatives to testing by experience, and no real discussion or revision of beliefs was possible in an age when acts of faith were elevated to absolute truth. Fixed conclusions turned disagreement into heresy.

Mere freedom of expression, however, is no corrective to the abuses of the past, because freedom without responsibility is a waste of time. Since even modern, "sophisticated," liberal theologians resist the idea that the existence, nature, and power of God are empirical questions, theology is profitably dispensed with. A "science" that has no adequate technique for distinguishing between reality and creative fiction beyond the presence of inner certainty may provide short-run therapy but hardly long-run usefulness.

2. The derivative powers of modern education are the result of intellectual fearlessness. Jewish anti-idolatry carried to its logical conclusion means that there is no word, idea, hypothesis, or value which a man should be afraid to reject. It also means that there is no person, place, thing, or force which a man should be afraid to investigate or measure.

However, traditional religion thrived on the category of sacredness. Sacred persons, objects, or ideas are "taboo," dangerous to investigate and absolutely non-rejectable. The appropriate response to sacredness is not measured probing; it is the act of worship. Worship is an awesome adoration which precludes sober investigation. When a worshipper lacks information about the object of his reverence, he generally replies, "It's a mystery," (with all its implications of the dangerous unknown). When a scientist lacks information about the object of his research, he usually replies, "I don't know," (with all its aura of pedestrian sobriety).

In an age when man has replaced worship with the techniques of analysis and free inquiry, the category of the sacred is inappropriate. Scientific man, on the basis of research, may respect persons, values, and ideas, but he cannot adore them.

The problem with theology and the whole notion of God is

that the object of investigation is simultaneously an object of worship. How can one ever secure accurate and useful information about man's relationship to a supposed deity if the object of study requires the mood of reverence and the attitude of awe? Theology, by its very nature, violates the conditions under which investigation is valid. "God" as a kind of personified sacredness is not divorceable from worship. Theology, therefore, reveals no information about the power structure of the universe; it merely inhibits proper inquiry and romanticizes ignorance.

3. One of the many justifications proposed for a theistic religion is that without God as the author of morality, there can be no valid or effective basis for traditional social ethics. If kindness, truth-telling, loyalty, and love are only cultural conventions or human options, then, in the absence of state coercion, what possible motivation exists for the compelling nature of moral behavior? Without God to lend sanction to ethical precepts, there can be neither ethics nor precepts.

The fallacy in this reasoning is obvious. First, it is an "odd" sociological fact that the "divine" commandments of a culture seem to correspond to the prevailing moral standards and alter as the culture alters. If divine sanction has been attached to what we presently regard as morally commendable, it has more frequently been attached to what is morally reprehensible. The problem with so much historic antisemitism, race hatred, blood warfare, and deprivation of liberty is that it has been tied up with "God's will." Divine sanction, as a morals enforcer, has historically caused as much social harm as social good, and aggravated the problem by making objectionable behavior sacred. The enemies of the prophets, as well as the prophets, loved to cite the untestable approval of the Deity.

Secondly, the ethical "authority" of God is derived from his supposed power and intention. To assert that God commands a particular behavioral procedure is in itself to provide no motivation for doing the action. For one may reasonably ask, "Why ought I to obey God?" The traditional reply was twofold: God rewards obedience and punishes disobedience; and God is both supremely wise and benevolent. The former reply finds its ultimate authority in man's desire for happiness and the consequent wish to avoid punishment; the second reply assumes that if the observer is able to describe God as desiring good, he already knows what "good" is before he so describes God. If, in a rational age, it is no longer possible to believe in a celestial policeman, the "ethical" authority of God is nil.

And, thirdly, what is conducive to human happiness is not a function of cultural whim and human option. It is an empirical question that depends on the accurate observation of human nature and enviroment. The correctness of an ethical procedure is testable by its consequence on human satisfaction and frustration. If the psychological and social sciences have been morally weak guides up to now, it is largely owing to the prevailing "religious" myth that values are distinct from the informational sciences. Too many people confuse the difficulty of empirically handling value questions with the impossibility of doing so.

4. The prevailing attitude in educated circles toward matters theological is vast indifference. The mystic's fondness and the atheist's hatred are absent. (While many people are aroused by the "God is Dead" controversy, they are attracted more by the social non-conformity than the theological shock.) If we assume that this indifference is the result of spiritual insensitivity to vital information, we will misunderstand. The truth of the matter is that the indifferent are not quite sure that theologians are giving them any information at all.

This problem highlights the whole question of truth. Before a statement can be evaluated as true or false, the assertion must be meaningful; it must make sense. If I utter, "Scubbish-mubbish," and ask you to tell me whether it is true or false, you would reply, "Impossible, I don't know what you're talking about."

Now most ordinary conversations about "God" are meaningful. They concern a heavenly father-figure with a distinct personality who is capable of the full range of human sensation and emotion and who possesses immense power to execute his desire. While one may not presently be able to directly verify his existence, one can imagine the conditions (in this life or the next) under which such an encounter would be possible. Although a rational age has made such a God an impossible attachment to admit to, the assertion of his existence has at least one virtue—it may be false, but at least it is meaningful. The fundamentalist may utter naïve absurdities, yet he never suffers from the "sophisticated" disease of preferring vagueness to clarity. An anthropomorphic God has the delightful advantage over most other varieties of simply being conceivable.

In an age when all scientific disciplines from physics to psychology seek to make their concepts and language more precise, the theologian alone reverses the procedure. While in Biblical times statements about God were fairly clear and specific, today analytic precision in theological matters is regarded as childish. While all other sources of useful power are subjected to increasing human measurement, divine power recedes into a protective realm "beyond space and time" where mortal hands can never defile it. In classical theology the most profound concepts are always the most nebulous and vague; to have any specific image of God is to hold a primitive notion.

Medieval and modern "liberal" theologians are the most guilty of providing non-information. To define God as "ultimate reality," "necessary existence," or "ground of being" is to utter pretty phrases but to do no more than that. In order for a statement to be meaningful, one must be able to conceive the evidence which would prove it true and the evidence which would prove it false. If it is not possible to imagine any situation which would prove it false (i.e., if it is protected by definition from all possible refutation), it is either trivial or nonsensical. The three definitions cited above exemplify this fault; they border on "Scubbish-mubbish."

For those theologians who discard the ordinary meaning

of the word "God" and identify it with some natural object, feeling, or value, their problem is providing pseudo-information about the world. Certainly "God is Love" provides no more information than does "Love is Love"; nor does "God is Nature" say any more than "Nature is Nature." To equate an historic person-word with perfectly adequate thing-words is to abuse language and invite confusion.

All that the theological naturalist ends up doing is absurdly talking to "Love" and talking to "Nature." These awkward definitions prompt a question: Why should perfectly rational human beings, who have at their disposal a host of English words more adequate than "God" to describe the natural events they are interested in, feel emotionally compelled to rip a three-letter word out of its historic context in order to save it for their belief vocabulary?

The reality of the theological situation for hosts of common-sensical people is that God "died" a long time ago. It is the word "God" with all its overtones of social respectability and ancestral approval that survives for graduates of the "university" religion.

If, then, man is to appropriately answer the age-old religious question: "How do I adequately relate to the extraordinary powers of the universe in order to achieve my salvation?", he must discard the colossal wasteland of theology and turn to a study of those realistic powers that most dramatically affect his future. It seems to me that the most significant religious discipline of modern times would be anthropology, the study of man in his totality. For it is empirically obvious that the most effective and available powers for human happiness are man's reason and man's love. To understand their origin, nature, and potential is the primary task of modern religion.

The Bible

A discussion group was recently established in a local

Jewish women's charity society. Considerable reflection was devoted to the topics and literature to be studied. Although there was a vague feeling that something contemporary would be most appropriate to the interests and reading taste of the membership, the overwhelming sentiment confirmed the decision that "since they were Jewish, they ought to know more about their Bible." The inevitable consequence was that another Bible study group, imbued with a sense of patriotic devotion to the past, was added to the endless roster of Scripture classes that fill the landscape of Jewish suburban culture.

Now a decision to study the Bible or any famous book out of the Jewish past is most commendable. Certainly, it would be difficult to understand the origins and early development of Jewish customs and institutions without a familiar use of this early literature. The overwhelming commitment of Jewish piety in the years before the Emancipation was, with good reason, to Scriptural commentary and its derivative legal literature. In a cultural milieu where the Torah reigned supreme in more than a figurative sense no other procedure was morally possible.

But, today, the obsessive interest in the Jewish religion school and adult education programs with Bible heroes, Scriptural interpretation, and Biblical archeology is an almost absurd affection. In a secular environment, where this Hebrew anthology has ceased to function in any realistic way as the supreme arbiter of thought and behavior, the choice to commit the limited amount of time available for religious study to the unraveling of Biblical "mysteries" is to exclude the possibility of getting to know alternative literature. Countless hours are devoted by talented clergymen to demonstrate how texts which appear to be both historically hythical and ethically irrelevant are, in reality, earth-shakingly significant. Why modern literature which expresses their sentiments more directly is less desirable for immediate study appears initially puzzling.

Liberal Jewish study programs are, to a large extent, unimaginative. They are the function of inertia and the guilt-feeling that allows the opposition to define what is religiously important. They also operate within the environment of a Protestant culture which regards the Bible as the greatest of all possible books and as representative of the only significant episodes in Jewish history. Whatever Jews did and said before the advent of Jesus is gigantic in import and worthy of a cinema cast of thousands; whatever they became afterwards is religiously irrelevant unless, like the State of Israel, the scenery has to do with the Holy Land. The fascination of Jews with the Dead Sea Scrolls cannot be justified either by their inspirational content or their historical wonder. (They are intellectually comparable to the religious pronouncements of some of the more bizarre sects of southern California.) It can only be explained by an American Jewish desire to identify with historical moments which small-town Christian culture deems important.

We are to a large extent the prisoners of our interfaith goodwill. Eager to please and to find acceptance in an American culture that worshiped the Bible, we have insisted on passing ourselves off as the People of the Book, and the devotees of Biblical piety. Our defense mechanism against antisemitism is to plead the endorsement of the 'Old Testament' and to identify the modern Jew with all those simple patriarchs, Bedouin figures, and shepherd kings that Christians adore. One of the supreme ironies of American religious life is that the one group who through urbanized sophistication are now most divorced from the belief framework and behavior patterns of the Scriptural milieu are the most eager to plead Biblical virtue. To the liberal American Jew, the Bible is not merely a record of how early Jews felt and believed; on that level it would not deserve one-half the concern lavished on it. Nor is it the major source of the contemporary Jew's religious information or inspiration; if that were so, rabbis would not have to devote lecture after lecture, book after book, and class after class to "proving" its significance. Its power derives from its social setting. It happens to be the Jewish book the Gentile world likes most. It is, therefore, our supreme ego defense and our passport to religious respectability. The American Jewish concentration on Biblical study to the virtual exclusion of contemporary Jewish literature has certain harmful e ʾects that prevent a viable and effective Judaism from emerging. These effects are itemized in the following observations.

1. Contemporary official Jewish publication is still overwhelmingly apologetic, geared to convince Bible-believing Christians of Jewish worth and significance. American Judaism has a defensive quality that devours the easy 'compliments' of a James Michener and Max Dimont and resists the sober reality of modern Jewish belief and behavior. So long as Jews deem it socially necessary to indicate that they and the Pilgrims are religious twins, so long will organized Jewish religion of the liberal variety condemn itself to a wilderness of arid Biblical scholarship and the amused indifference of the secular and scientific world that claims our Jewish youth. Platitudes about the whole Bible being summed up in the Ten Commandments may give our behavior a tenuous connection with Levitical and prophetic teaching, but it only sums up the basic ethical irrelevance of the rest.

2. A proper understanding and appreciation of the Bible is not possible until one is able to divorce it from Jewish ego needs and view it as a historical document that need not reflect our own beliefs and attitudes but *did* express the collective and often opposed views of our ancestors in the days of the First and Second Temples. In order to understand what we Jews *are* in the twentieth-century we ought to thoroughly study our origins and so be aware of the early experiences that helped to mold the character traits of our social personality. But no objective study of these Biblical origins is possible if we feel compelled to *defend* the Bible or to prove that the writers *really* meant to say is what we believe today.

3. Most post-Biblical literature is indeed Bible oriented. The Midrash, the Talmud, and the medieval philosophic writings rely heavily on Biblical quotations and per-

petually explain and clarify Scriptural verses. No other dependence is conceivable in an age which deemed the Torah a revealed constitution. But the connection is deceptive. In reality, the Biblical quotations are mere pretexts, twisted out of their historical contexts to justify change, innovation, and popular custom. What is most interesting about post-Biblical rabbinic literature is not its artificial connection with Biblical law and history, but its natural connection with the contemporary environment out of which it emerged. Biblical authority was important to the rabbis who preached; but, in reality, it was not something to be learned from; it was something to be used, a power to be invoked for the justification of conclusions the social environment had already dictated. Undue concentration on the Bible hides the true source of rabbinic decision and ethics.

4. An appropriate Judaism must deal with the Jew as he really *is*, not as ancient literature conceived him. Since the modern Jew is the supreme product of urban living, his most significant religious literature ought to reflect this fact. Post-Emancipation Jewry, along with most of Western culture, underwent a revolutionary change in its almost total identification with the industrial city. This trauma is reflected today in the obvious truth that socially, economically, and technically our European great-grandfathers were closer to Rabbi Akiba eighteen centuries earlier than to us. Undue emphasis on the Bible distorts the nature of Jewish identity and living in the twentieth century. Shepherd patriarchs, Bedouin sheikhs, and country prophets are incongruous authority figures in the age of the urban technician and professional. If the Jews like the Amish were still identified with rural 'virtues', the Biblical emphasis might be tolerable. But the contrary is true. Of all things, the Jew is *most* identified with the citified professional. In contemporary America, the Bible becomes nothing more than charming nostalgia; it cannot help the Jew deal with his social reality. The economics and social relations of the East European *shtetl* might have had some

remote connection with the Biblical setting. Modern New York has none at all.

5. Religious school curricula in liberal synagogues and temples ought to expose the student to important Biblical figures. But they ought to avoid making these personalities the supreme examples of Jewish virtue and intelligence. As has happened in the Christian churches, Sunday School has too often turned into Bible story time. The child is exposed to a continuing series of personalities and events that bears little relationship to his own experience. Unless the genuine character of the 'hero' is distorted and violence is done to historical truth, the herdsman patriarch of Genesis is no real competition for the T.V. scientist, and the shepherd soldier of Samuel runs a poor second to the astronaut. It may very well be true that if George Washington and Abraham Lincoln with all their embarrassing 'newness' can serve as contemporary heroes for little children, Sigmund Freud, Albert Einstein, and Theodore Herzl might even do better ethically and emotionally than Jephtha and Sampson. Little Sigmund at least lived in a city despite his Oedipus Complex; and little Albert hated war even as a child.

Historically, the Bible has dominated the lesson parts of the Sabbath and holiday liturgy. Year after year the continuous Torah cycle repeats itself in synagogues committed to liberalism with no apparent signs of relief. Talented little Barmitsvah boys arise to recite to Reform congregations the recipe for incense or the requirements for priestly ablutions. Even if the consecutive weekly readings are abandoned and the lessons are chosen by topic from the Bible, the range of lesson literature is confined to a set of documents edited and censored by Levitical priests, and expressive of a dogmatic world view that for all practical purposes died with the rise of rabbinic Judaism. No historical nostalgia can justify that perpetual waste of a congregation's time. A creative liturgy would select ethical and philosophic lessons, both ancient and modern, that are both lucid, directly applicable, and intellectually respectable. Why is the pedestrian work of a fifth-century Jerusalem

priest to be preferred as a Sabbath lesson to the poetry
of Martin Buber?

The alternative to Biblical lessons is *not* rabbinic literature. In many respects the observations of Talmudic and
medieval writers are considerably more sophisticated than
the perceptions of Biblical authors; but they are no more
expressive of the thought patterns and world outlook of the
modern Western Jew than their Bible predecessors. Since
Jewish identity in European and American culture is no
longer a function of belief or ritual commitment, but rather
of birth and historical memory, the criterion for Jewish
literature cannot be conformity to a certain set of ideas or
loyalty to a particular linguistic tradition. In a society
which cherishes the basic necessity of free inquiry, Jewish
writing is the literary product of anyone who is born into
the social identity of being Jewish. The self-awareness that
arises from this condition, whether articulated or not, is the
single factor that unites this body of writing and identifies
the Jewish writer.

The literary works of Sigmund Freud, Erich Fromm,
Marcel Proust, Franz Kafka, Isaiah Berlin, and Sidney
Hook, for all their apparent topical diversities and universal relevance, are products of persons who share the
Jewish social "fate"; and, therefore, are as expressive of the
twentieth-century Jewish reality as Isaac Singer or Agnon.
A religious society that purports to reveal the role of the
Jewish people in the modern world will prefer their words to
merely ancient ones. To the Jew of the post-Emancipation
world the Bible may serve his need for historical pride; but a
viable Judaism must help him relate effectively to the real
flesh and blood people who share his 'destiny'. Erich
Fromm may indeed be a better object of study for a Jewish
study group than the Book of Genesis. Outside the romance
of venerability, he is a much more effective expression of
what we are, feel, and really desire to be.

Our conclusion is simple. The 'sacred' literature of
Judaism must reflect the reality of Jewish life and belief. It
must be a faithful record of the social and scientific

revolution that has transformed the Jewish mind and made the Bible a book of primarily historical interest.

Religion

In recent years I have encountered a persistent objection to the vocabulary of Humanistic Judaism. Many perceptive and sensitive observers have affirmed the values of the Temple philosophy and program. They readily acknowledge that the group work and fellowship are meaningful experiences. But they counter with the objection, "How can you call your organization a Temple?" Humanism may be a 'great' philosophy of life. It may even be the ideological answer to man's twentieth century needs. Yet, if there is one thing it isn't, it isn't a religion. If you are so concerned about the meticulous use of vocabulary that you abstain from God-language, why then would you not be equally careful with the word 'religion'?

The question is a significant one. If we are going to designate our philosophy and institution as religious, then we must be as precise and accurate with the phrases we employ as we expect the theologian to be with the words he uses. After all, there is something called the ethics of words! · One has a moral obligation to be faithful to the historic meaning of ordinary words.

Now to discover the authentic significance of 'religion', we must clarify the unique characteristics of the religious experience. It will not do to either arbitrarily pick a definition that is convenient to one's vested interest or to cite those qualities of the experience that it shares with other human possibilities. A proper definition must rely on what is peculiar to the event under analysis. Nor will selecting a vague phrase that makes 'religion' the sum total of everything promote understanding. To define religion as 'the pursuit of fulfillment' or 'the pursuit of salvation' or 'the act of relating to the universe as a whole' is to consign the term to the limbo of words that have lots of prestige but refer to nothing in particular. For after all, what human activity from psychiatry to politics is not concerned with human fulfillment? And what human procedure does not involve relating to the universe 'as a whole'?

Initially we must do away with the verbal debris; we must clarify what religion is *not*. Many liberals are fond of designating the religious experience as the moral dimension of human life, as the ethical commitment of the individual. However, while it is certainly true that all historic religions have been vitally concerned with social right and wrong, it is also true that there are hosts of activities, normally designated as religious, that have nothing at all to do with ethical propriety. Lighting candles and celebrating spring festivals are a part of piety and are morally neutral. Moreover, large numbers of sincere and sensitive people think of themselves and are regarded by others as both ethical and non-religious.

Many popular definers prefer to associate religion with the act of faith as opposed to the procedures of empirical reasoning. Religion is viewed as a unique approach to questions of truth. While this definition may attract by its simplicity, it will not "hold water." Certainly the act of reasoning through observable evidence is common to parts of all sacred scriptures; and the procedure of intuitive trust in the truthfulness of self-proclaimed authorities is as common to the daily procedures of politics and business as it is to those endeavors that are normally regarded as religious.

As for the persistent attempts to identify religion with the worship of God, they may be appropriate within the narrow framework of Western culture but they are invalid universally. The Confucian ethical tradition and the Buddhist Nirvans are religiously as significant as God and yet are quite distinct from the normal notion of deity. Nor will the Julian Huxley definition of the religious experience as the apprehension of the sacred quite do. To simply describe the sacred as that which is able to arouse awe, wonder, and reverence is to identify its consequences but not to clarify the nature of its constituent parts. Without analysis the definition simply substitutes one mystery for another.

A proper view of religion requires an honest confrontation with certain historical realities. Too often clerical liberals choose to designate what is 'unpleasant' about traditional religious practice as secondary and peripheral. They refuse to confront the possibility that what they stand for may in any way be 'less religious' than what the traditionalists proclaim. In a culture where to be 'more religious' is to be more respectable, the refusal is understandable although it is hardly conducive to an objective study of religion.

What are the historical realities which our study cannot ignore? Six facts are most significant.

1. In almost every culture religious institutions are the most conservative. It is historically demonstrable that ecclesiastical procedures change more slowly than other social patterns. Ideas which are regarded as radical and revolutionary within the framework of church and synagogue are usually regarded as commonplace in other areas of human behavior. While most institutions resist change, organized religion has been the most supportive of the status quo. Intrinsic to established 'priesthoods' is the notion that change may be necessary but not desirable.

2. Religious teachers and prophets persistently refuse to admit that their ideas are new. If they do, the indispensable sacred character of their revelations disappears. From Moses to Bahaullah the religious radical must always demonstrate that he is, in reality, the most genuine of conservatives. Moses pleaded the endorsement of Abraham; Jesus insisted that he was but the fulfiller of old prophecies. Mohammed posed as the reviver of pure monotheism, and Luther claimed that he desired only to restore the pristine and authentic Christianity. As for Confucius, he denied originality and attributed all his wisdom to old emperors. Even the Jewish Reformers vehemently affirmed that they were guilty of no basic novelty but were simply recapturing the true message of the true Prophets. No historic religious

'genius' has ever desired to claim a new idea. Change is made to appear an illusion. 'New' concepts are either old ones long forgotten or old ones reinterpreted. Novelty is historically irreligious.

3. In ordinary English the word 'religious' is usually equivalent to the Yiddish 'frumm'. Both adjectives are tied up with the notion of ritualism. An individual is judged as 'more religious' or 'less religious' by the degree of his ritual behavior. The liberal may protest that this usage is narrow and primitive. But he still has to explain why even sophisticated speakers, when they relax with the word 'religious' and are non-defensive, choose to associate it with repetitive ceremonies.

4. The annual cycle of seasons, as well as the life cycle of human growth and decay, are universal concerns of all organized religions. Spring and puberty may have no apparent ethical dimension, but they are certainly more characteristic of historic religious interest than social action. We may deplore the religious obsession with Barmitsvah. But then, after all, we have to explain it.

5. Despite Whitehead's popular definition of religion as that which man does with his solitude, most religious activities have to do with group action. In most cultures sacred events are not separable from either family loyalty or national patriotism. The very word 'religio' is a Roman term for the sum of public ceremonies that express the allegiance of the citizen to the state. Even the ancestor cult which defines the popular religion of most of the Eastern world is an act of group loyalty that diminishes the significance of the isolated individual and enhances the importance of family continuity. Historic religion started with the group and is not easily separable from it.

6. The notion of the saint or the holy man permeates most religious cultures. This revered individual achieves his status not only because of his impeccable ritual and moral behavior but also because he is able to enjoy the summit of the religious experience. To be able to transcend this messy world of space-time change and to unite

mystically with what is beyond change, space, and time is his special forte. The mystic experience has almost universally been regarded as the supreme religious event and the entree into the supernatural.

Any adequate theory about the nature of the religious experience and its unique characteristics must be able to explain these six facts. It must find the common cord that binds these disparate events together. While many factors can account for some of them, only one theory takes care of all of them. And this theory is inseparable from the initial concern of historic philosophy.

It is interesting to note that the origin of philosophic inquiry and metaphysics lies in a disdain for the sensible world of continual change and in a persistent love of what is eternal and beyond decay. Plato was adored by later theologians because of his 'religious' temperament. He detested the world of impermanence and asserted that wisdom was only concerned with entities that never change. The chaotic world of space-time events which modern science investigates was anathema to his pursuit of knowledge. If the Greeks were unable to develop the rudiments of a real empiricism, herein lay their problem. Whatever they searched for had to be deathless and eternal.

In fact, the search for the deathless is the psychic origin of the religious experience. The human individual is a unique animal. He alone is fully aware of his personal separateness from other members of his species and conscious of the temporary nature of his own existence. He fears death and often needs to believe that dying is an illusion. In his anxiety he probes the world for persons and forces which enjoy the blessing of immortality. With these he seeks to identify and to find the thrill of being part of something 'bigger than me'. The religious experience is universally a feeling of being 'at one with' what seems to possess the aura of eternity. This definition works superbly to show the essentially conservative nature of historic religion. Change, experiment, and mere opinion are in spirit nonreligious. Only eternal truths will do. All seeming change is pure illusion, and even the most radical steps must be covered up by the cloak of 'reinterpretation'. The definition also clarifies why all new truths must be labelled as old. The religious temperament requires the solace of age, and venerability. Even if the good word is humanly new, it turns out to be 'divinely old'.

The theory explains the religious power of ritual. Traditional ceremony is not significant because of its ethical symbolism; that excuse is a sop for the modern intellect. Ritual acts derive their psychic punch from the fact that they are meticulously identical and repetitive. In a world of continual and frightening change they give to human behavior the feeling of eternity. Their power is not symbolic; it is intrinsic to the ceremony itself. New observances that are labelled as new may be aesthetically charming, but they lack the religious dimension. As for the seasons and life-cycle events, what greater evidence is required to substantiate the thesis? Societies may undergo revolutions and violent social upheaval; they may experience the overthrow of every existing value and idea. But the explosion is powerless to alter the relentless sequence of spring, summer, fall, winter—birth, puberty, maturity, and death. Nothing is more 'eternal' than the seasons. Their continual repetition is an ultimate 'security'.

Moreover, the group character of most religious observance reflects the human desire for permanence. The family and the nation have always been inseparable from the major religious experiences of any culture, simply because they suggest the immortality the individual does not. And the mystic experience is equally explained by this need to defeat change and death. The ecstasy of the 'saint' is rationalized as an encounter with the changeless. To 'transcend' the world of space and time may be informationally absurd, but as an exclamation of victory over the fear of death it has emotional significance.

If then the unique character of the religious experience is the act of identifying with what appears to be 'permanent', a proper understanding of humanism requires the following observations.

1. The religious temperament and the pursuit of knowledge through empirical procedures are incompatible. Humanism is committed to the techniques of modern science, and all proper statements within the framework are tentative, subject to the refutation of future evidence. Empiricism cannot tolerate eternal truths about man and the universe. The conditional character of all knowledge with an infinite capacity for adjustment is its special power and glory. Whenever the religious need and the pursuit of truth come together there is disaster. The Greeks prove that point magnificently: they could never end up being interested in what was tentative and conditional.

2. Humanism is a total philosophy of life, which does not allow the religious temperament to invade every area of its discipline. However, there is one aspect of living where religion is indispensable. If man has a need to transcend his temporariness and identify with something or someone more permanent than the individual 'I', this need cannot be ignored. Within the framework of humanism, two ways of satisfaction exist. By asserting that every man is composed of the same matter that all other events in the universe derive from, humanistic teaching affirms that each of us shares an intimate bond, a basic identity, with any conceivable happening in this universe. Stars and flowers are material brothers to our nature. And by proclaiming that before and beyond the individuality of any person each of us shares an essential oneness with all men, humanism proclaims that all of us individually share in the immortality of mankind as a whole. In fact, the very basis of ethical behavior lies in this religious experience. If every person can view only himself as an individual, the social character of morality is impossible. Ethical behavior is only feasible when men sense that the essential nature that binds them together is more significant than the individual differences that separate them.

3. Humanism is *more* than a religion. There are certain areas of its discipline which provide the religious experi-

ence, there are many involvements where the religious temperament is either irrelevant or harmful. In opposition to the temper of much traditional philosophy where the mood of 'eternity' pervades, humanism affirms the value of conditional knowledge and change. Therefore, the humanist never regards the description 'less religious' as a threat. He rather views it as a compliment. He is aware of the fact that the balanced life requires much more. While he resists the invasion of all of life by the religious temperament, he, at the same time, affirms the value of the religious experience in the simple rehearsal of nature's seasons and in the image of immortality in mankind's survival.

Jewishness First

A dialogue was held in Jerusalem between American Jewish students and their Israeli counterparts on the subject of Jewish survival. The record of the discussion was recently published and reveals the barren character of these exhanges. The Israelis typically charged the Americans with choosing to live in an environment less Jewish than Israel, while the American students countered with a defensive affirmation that "one can be as Jewish in the United States as in Israel." As the verbal assaults increased in intensity, the arguments degenerated into the usual apologetics, where each side asserted its right to the title of "maximal Judaism."

The Jerusalem discussion highlights one of the major difficulties of our intrafaith dialogue. Every group, whether conservative, liberal, or radical, must confess its equal attachment to the preservation of Judaism and the survival of Jewishness.

The historic founders of classical Reform vehemently denied that, by dispensing with the vast majority of traditional ritual practice, their followers were less Jewish than the most ardent Orthodox, or that Judaism could be parochially equated with Hebrew or Yiddish. They asserted that they were simply reviving the old message of the prophets, the *true* Judaism which had long been obscured by ceremonial trivia. The person who conscientiously observed the ethical norms of the prophetic word was equally as Jewish, if not more so, than the pious old man who devoted his energies and anxieties to the meticulous detail of the dietary laws.

Our Conservative school has been equally aggressive in its assertions of "authentic" Judaism. To adjust to the "catholic" will of the people of Israel, even though it meant dispensing with a few rituals, was much more the "historical" Judaism than appearances would indicate. To embrace the gradual evolution of religious idea and form is to suddenly find oneself more Jewish than the reactionary. The Diaspora non-Zionist plays the same game. He vigorously affirms that his theological beliefs and ethical practices give him a life as profoundly Jewish as any non-religious Israeli steeped in Hebrew culture.

But the modernist defense is a shallow one, because it denies the obvious. If an activity is to be an adequate expression of Jewish identity, it must be easily recognized as being Jewish by both the performer and the observer. A value or moral procedure which is practiced or indulged by mankind in general is less than effective in creating a sense of conspicuous difference. Being nice to a neighbor, giving generously to charity, emphasizing the importance of education, or just loving the family, are all commendable and Jewish but not exclusively so. They are certainly less self-consciously Jewish than keeping kosher, observing Rosh Hashanah, or praying in Hebrew.

The problem with identifying Jewishness with certain theological beliefs or moral doctrines is that the religionist is hard put to find any acceptable beliefs or doctrines that are uniquely Jewish. Aside from the Orthodox commitment to the idea that God commanded certain specific ritual practices, there are very few notions that have any touch of unique Monotheism; reward and punishment, divine mercy and justice, are now clichéd adjuncts of a dozen historic

religions. To counter this threatening universality, Reform
was driven to do two things: to indulge the childish and
irrelevant game of "we said it first"; and to promote the one
surviving doctrine that had any semblance of uniqueness,
the idea that Jews were especially chosen to set some sort of
moral example to the rest of the world. The ironic fact that
any people claiming to be a moral example lacked the very
quality of humility which would enable them to become one
escaped the Reform theologians, so desperate were they for
some doctrine that was distinctively Jewish. Even today,
although it is more than obvious that the notion has elicited
no real conviction from the Jewish masses, it is obsessively
clung to as the one last claim to a Hebrew exclusive.

In the realm of ethical values, one repeatedly hears
educators and rabbis singing the praises of Jewish values.
But, again, if one excludes the attachment to certain
ceremonial forms, there are no significant moral commitments that are uniquely Jewish, either in belief, practice, or
origin. If we cite devotion to family, the Greeks, Armenians,
Italians, and Chinese provide embarrassing competition;
and if we cite the love of education the Scots and the
Japanese are passionate duplicates. Even with our vaunted
patronage of learning, we are forced to admit that the
Greeks had more to do with the creation of the modern
secular university than our own tradition. Moreover, while
the pursuit of social justice is a religious must, it will never
heighten Jewish self-consciousness. It will simply expose
us to millions of people who share our values and have
derived them from sources different from our own.

The "painful" truth is that our Jewish distinctiveness lies
in no real separation of belief and moral ideal; it finds its
definition in the "trivia" of ceremony and language. One
truth is undeniable: Hebrew is uniquely Jewish. Plato in
Hebrew is more easily identified as a Jewish event than
Hillel's golden rule in English; and Israeli poetry about the
stars is more quickly recognized as Jewish literature than
Kaufman Kohler's German discourses on the divine. In a
very real sense American Judaism is less Jewish than

Israeli culture. It is bound to be. When one is dealing with
the expression of universal sentiments and values, then the
linguistic medium is the only distinction.

By the same criterion, Reform is less Jewish than
Orthodoxy. Traditional Jews obviously do more uniquely
Jewish activity than the liberals, with or without being
ethical exemplars. Long discourses on the "mainstream"
and "the motivating force of Jewish history" will never
obscure the reality of the difference. To any fairly common-
sensical observer, Reform promotes fewer activities that are
easily identified by doer or see-er as Jewish than its
Orthodox counterpart.

The problem of the modern religionist is not that he is
less Jewish and prefers to be less Jewish than his forefathers; it is his frightened embarrassment at having to
admit it. Many a liberal rabbi has to exhaust himself with
devious apologetics to demonstrate to his congregation,
that, although they have abandoned the conspicuous and
defining behavior of the Jew, they are *really* as Jewish as
all those "false pietists" who identify religion with ritual.
The harassed Reform Jew, when confronted with the
accusation of a diluted Judaism, protests with angry
statements about "what is really important in religion." He
functions with the premise that to be "less Jewish" is
sinful.

Here lies the mistake and fault of so many liberal
apologists. Instead of freely admitting, "Yes, we are less
Jewish—now what?"; they deny the reality of motive and
deed and proceed to defend what is indefensible. The truth
of the matter is that liberal Judaism is a new historic
affirmation of the fact that the modern Jew has found
religious values more important than Jewishness. If this
were not the case, Reform would long since have embraced
Zionism or the ghetto. Williamsburg and Tel Aviv are much
more effective than the average suburban temple for the
maximizing of identifiable Jewish activity.

For many Jews, Jewishness is the primary value. All
other concerns are subordinate. These are the friends of my

youth who sacrificed the comforts of their American home to pioneer a new land where Hebrew culture would be a living reality. These are my contemporaries, sensitive and sentimental, who are "devout" members of Orthodox and Conservative synagogues, and who by education and belief are totally divorced from the ideology they mouth, but who sincerely feel that doing things Jewish is worth the sacrifice of intellectual integrity. The dilemma of the Reconstructionist is precisely this. For he is asking, "How can I say all the old words that are distinctively Jewish, and yet not really mean them?"

But for the vast majority of the Jews in America this commitment to maximal Jewishness is purely verbal. Not because they are too weak and too lazy to practice what they preach; but because they are too embarrassed to preach what they practice—to articulate what they genuinely believe. They have acquired the values of individualism and universalism and yet feel treasonous to say so, unless they can prove that their open-mindedness is as Jewish as Yom Kippur. They have embraced the ideal of a public and scientific education with the distinct advantage of English-speaking culture and yet feel guilty of uttering this view unless some clergyman can sanction their value by showing that ethics in English is as Jewish as matza. But the pretense is too painful and exhausting to last, and exposes the rabbinate to justifiable ridicule.

If Jews are to survive in America, they must be willing to admit that the performance of identifiable Jewish activity is important, but that it is not as important as the expression of other religious values. The liberal temple must enable its members to relax with their Jewishness, not make them tense over its defense. It must be willing to proclaim, without shame or regret, but with the pride of conviction, that it has an obligation to promote not only Jewish identity but also other social ideals. The irony of the twentieth century is that in order for Christianity to survive it must do fewer things that are uniquely Christian; and in order for Judaism to survive it must direct its energies to what is not uniquely Jewish, but to what is common and universal.

Nostalgia

In his book, *The Territorial Imperative,* Robert Ardrey described the bizarre spawning habits of a nesting colony of green sea-turtles. The female members of the species leave the lush jungle of the Brazilian shore, travel 1400 miles across the fierce waters of the South Atlantic, and infallibly arrive at an almost invisible dot of land called Ascension Island. There they lay their eggs and return across the choppy seas to Brazil. This reproductive drama is repeated year after year with unfailing accuracy.

Green sea-turtles "suffer" from a genetic disposition called *nostalgia*—the Greek way of saying "homesickness." Despite the obvious advantages of their local habitat, the animals succumb to an overpowering urge to return to the site of their infancy. The instinct for home overrides every other desire and drives them irresistibly to their native land. Innate and childhood memories merge to enforce a compulsive pattern.

While man is free of most of the behavior dictation that sea-turtles have to endure, he is not free of nostalgia. Like some venerable antique which can no longer perform its original function, it persists in the human psyche. No longer conferring any reproductive advantage, it turns the mind of man to the scenes of his childhood and to the native habitat of his family.

Certainly, no area of human life enjoys the tyranny of nostalgia more than the realm of religion. Since religious ritual and mythology arose out of the tribal need to act out the conditions of group survival, they inevitably draw every receptive individual back to his tribal roots. As an activity which draws its basic psychic energy from an attachment to past events, religion is fertile ground for any nostalgic orgy and becomes the most respectable social vehicle for "going home."

The evidence for this assertion can readily be seen in Jewish behavior. While in recent years the rate of change in Jewish secular life has vastly increased, and while the social and intellectual milieu of the Jew is marked by a revolutionary difference from that of the past, the ritual pattern within the framework of the synagogue service has remained remarkably conservative. In fact, the Reform movement has restored to its worship service ritual items it had long since discarded; and hosts of Reform temples have now returned to regular readings of the Torah, Havdala ceremonies, and lengthy recitations of archaic liturgical Hebrew. In a world of monumental change, the temple remains the last convenient place where we can freely indulge our nostalgic urges without any serious disruption of our vital routine. The synagogue, objectively viewed as a social function, does not even have the reproductive usefulness of laying eggs.

As a human need, nostalgia cannot flippantly be ignored. Since the religious institution has historically chosen to meet this emotional demand it would be insensitive to ask it to abandon a social role it is so perfectly designed to perform. But if the modern temple has an additional function of greater importance—namely to enable each individual to dispel fantasy and to deal more realistically with his ethical decisions—then certain checks must be placed on nostalgic indulgence. To allow free run to "homesickness" in the religious milieu is to subvert the more productive opportunities of personal growth and to substitute the pleasant security of the tribal womb.

A healthy Jewish nostalgia avoids the following "pitfalls."

Idealizing the past. Jewish rabbinic authorities were generally prevented from making any useful and traditionally permissible changes by the doctrine of "steady deterioration." It was assumed that leaders of the present had no right to alter the decisions of leaders of the past because the wise men of the present could never be as wise as the scholars of the past. In learning, piety, and perception, advancing time always meant degeneration. "Things" were always getting worse. Only the dramatic intervention of the Messiah could reverse the trend.

While the modern Jew may publicly mock this view, his practical sentiment often indicates that he endorses it. Although he can readily see that the contemporary French constitution was a legal device of de Gaulle to enhance his presidential power, he finds it inconceivable that a normally ambitious Jewish priesthood created the Torah to enhance its own control. Although he despises the preacher personality of self-righteous fanatics, he finds in the message of the prophets (who were always consigning their enemies to some horrible, mutilating fate) the moral foundation of a humanistic civilization. A nostalgia that rips people and documents out of their historic context and de-normalizes them transforms the past from a useful reference into a useless shrine.

Missing the point. One of the conventional analyses of Jewish survival is that it is the product of theological commitment. The advocates of this view find the source of Jewish persistence in the Jewish belief in God. Without the concept of a personal deity who chose them as his special messengers, Jews would have lacked the collective will to live and would have ultimately fallen into the cultural stew of the ancient world. Since the attachment to God was the dynamic of Jewish survival, an attachment to the Jewish past demands a theological involvement. Whether the deity is imaginary or real is irrelevant; the belief in his special providence is the root of group endurance.

Such an analysis, unfortunately, distorts the past and misses reality. To the perceptive observer the theology of Israel is the conscious frosting on the unconscious cake. It is the trivial and respectable rationalization of feelings and thoughts that lie beneath the surface of Jewish awareness. It is not the case that God and the Exodus created Passover. Passover is older than Yahveh and the Exodus story; it has enjoyed many Jewish explanations throughout its long history. Ritual precedes mythology, and the tribal will to live precedes ritual. The concept of the chosen people is not the logical consequence of a belief in a universal deity; it is, rather, a clumsy camouflage for racial pride.

To be attached to the past is not merely to mouth the convenient verbal formulas of previous centuries. It is to sense the underlying currents of feeling that motivated their creation. Secular Zionism is as deeply nostalgic as theistic Reform—but with greater emotional bite. Although it discards theology and unashamedly proclaims its total reliance on human endeavor, it captures the mood of the past more effectively. In an age when God is irrelevant, the national will to live will find new reasons to justify its persistence. And, in an age when tribal feeling is less than respectable, Jewish intellectuals will find new ways to hide from Jews what they are embarrassed to verbalize. After all, what is wrong in admitting that "I like being part of an extended family." A worthwhile nostalgia begins with honesty.

Bad imitation. Loyalty to the personalities of our childhood has great emotional power. It is difficult to separate "bobe" and "zayde" from Seders, Kiddush cups, and Kol Nidre. Our memories of certain persons and events are all bound together by the pleasure of infant security and the irrational fear of reprisal. They resist dissection and prefer the vagueness of worship. In our adult life we seek to pay our tribute to these meaningful people of our past by doing the things they did, saying the things they said, and singing the songs they sang. As we go about our Jewish observance, we fantasize and imagine that they can see what we are doing and nod their approval.

But the imitation is usually awkward and lifeless. Our tribute lacks the emotional vitality of our childhood experience and has a shadowy character. Its failure lies in our lack of perception. When we imitate the symbol and not the substance, our loyalty is personally harmful. The special grace of our past is that the people who observed its rules did so with conviction and integrity. If they prayed, they believed in the power of prayer. If they fasted, they were convinced of the power of fasting. They were not actors in a play who know that every move is illusion; nor were they pretenders in a social drama, who require repeated assurances that what they are doing is really meaningful. To be loyal to the past is to find for oneself the integrity our ancestors found for themselves. It is to do, say, and sing whatever expresses our personal conviction. What was an outpouring of personal honesty for Rabbi Akiba is a charade for us. To recite the mourner's Kaddish without the theological conviction that gave it historic meaning is a travesty. It is an act of disrespect and a violation of loyalty.

Pretension. One of life's delightful experiences is to visit art museums. In the museum are all kinds of aesthetic and historical items which arouse our wonder and nostalgia. Whether they be products of American, Hindu, Egyptian, or Jewish culture; or whether they express sentiments and ideas we approve or disapprove of, we can admire the skill with which they were executed. We can also respond to the beauty with which they express convictions different from our own. Our role in the museum is that of an involved observer. It is similar to the function of an audience in the theater, or a browser in the library.

However, to turn a religious service into a museum in which a nostalgic audience sees and hears the superb aesthetic expressions of what their ancestors used to believe is to violate its better possibility. Undoubtedly, like good theater, it may invoke admiration and sympathy; but by treating the congregant as an emotional observer, it cheats him of ever being an effective participant.

Most Jewish services are elegant indulgences in pretentious nostalgia.

What else can explain the new Reform penchant for massive arks and luxuriously draped Torahs? The *beema* becomes a stage of museum magnitude in which detached observers come to view the relics of what their fathers used to believe. How can a Torah, whose intellectual framework and specific precepts have been overwhelmingly rejected by the behavior patterns of most liberal Jews, be an effective symbol of their philosophic commitment? A museum Judaism is a religion of shrines; it has nothing at all to do with making individuals confront the reality of themselves.

Avoiding the present. Religion has often been a haven from reality. In a world of relentless change, the synagogue and the church provided that center of permanence where nothing changed (neither words nor gestures) and where religious leaders brought comfort in their proclamation of "eternal truths." Those who most disliked the risk of time became the most religious, and those who feared novelty and surprise became the pious. If church institutions have become notorious bastions of conservative resistance, the development is understandable.

The emotional role of the synagogue in twentieth-century America is often the same one it performed in the Middle Ages. Since we live in a technological world where the rate of change is almost beyond human endurance, the need for a "haven of permanence" is intense. The function of the temple is to create a world of illusion in which the value of change is periodically applauded, but in which no significant change really occurs. While the sermons thunder the need for bold steps and courageous pioneering, the symbolism of ritual remains the same. Novelty and experiment are the stuff of the outside world; and the role of the synagogue is to shield us from its frightening uncertainty.

When nostalgia is the tool of fear, it weakens the people who use it and turns religious institutions into monasteries of illusion. A useful religion seeks to strengthen people; it enables them not only to admit change but to accept it emotionally. Nostalgia is only one of two emotional possibilities for Jews. The other is creativity. The second is harder, but ultimately more useful.

IV
COPING WITH REALITY

Identity

Jewishness is a modern paradox. While it is easy to define Jews it is hard to define what makes them Jewish. The criteria of identity are so unconscious that few people can articulate their standards. Although they are strong and compelling, verbal descriptions rarely do them justice. The state of Being Jewish seems to resist conventional categories and to emerge as a unique phenomenon.

Understanding the Jewish condition is inhibited by security needs. A minority vulnerable to hostility and persecution wants to create a public image of impeccable respectability. The religious definition of the Jew, which is the official "party" line of the community establishment, has less to do with the facts than with the need to conform socially. In a unitary American culture, which is intolerant of permanent ethnic diversity, Judaism must be essentially religious or forego its normality. After proper deference is paid to the propaganda of pluralism, lasting group loyalties which require neither church nor temple still appear as mildly subversive.

If we view religion narrowly as the organized expression of a theological point of view, or more broadly as a community reflection of a unique philosophy of life, then, in neither case, is the essence of contemporary Jewish identity religious. The metaphysical and ethical beliefs of American Jewry are as diverse as those of the general population. If the Lubavitcher Hasidim and the Workmen's Circle are part of the same group, then the group can hardly be defined by a single orientation to the cosmos. Membership in the community is pragmatically independent of either private belief or public creed.

The interfaith "what we Jews believe" syndrome is one of the more pathetic deceptions our culture provides. It hides the breadth of Jewish disagreement and obscures the real bonds of group identity.

Certainly, the racial definition of the Jew is less than appropriate. It has become almost a cliché of ADL propaganda to deny (with a host of scientific evidence) the myth of ethnic purity. Although Jews publicly resist genetic uniqueness, their private conversations about Jewish hereditary 'genius' reveals a viewpoint little different from the grosser racialism. Our people are ambivalent about physical identity; they like sharing the genes of Einstein as long as they can avoid any necessary connection with those of Fagin. When Kaufmann Kohler, the leader of Reform a half century ago, asserted that Jews possessed an innate gift for spiritual greatness, the Jews applauded. But Hitler and the antisemites changed the mood. Racial superiority was delightful; racial inferiority was less than tolerable.

It is undoubtedly true that, in given areas of the world, rigid inbreeding produced a regional Jewish 'type.' But there was no uniformity among the types. Modern Israel reveals the genetic diversity of world Jewry. The stark juxtaposing of European, Asiatic, and African Jews, so visible to the tourist eye, explodes the racial theory.

Cultural unity is no more adequate as a proper definition. Being an illusion, it survives in the dreams of secular chauvinists. Without having a Jewish language, Jewish citizens of Western technology tend to be indistinguishable from their middle-class neighbors. Israel's cultural uniqueness lies in the revival of the Hebrew language. Lived in English, Israeli life would become standard American.

If contemporary nationalists fight desperately for linguistic uniqueness, they do so because they know that, without it, assimilation to an international industrial culture is inevitable. Since Yiddish is dead and functional Hebrew is confined to a small minority of world Jewry, English speaking American Jews can share the society of their Anglo-Saxon colleagues more easily than the world of either their Russian relatives or their Israeli cousins.

Painting, music, and drama have also ceased to have clear national styles. The modern variations in artistic expression cross national boundaries and cause dissension within every country. Our present technology is molding an artistic smorgasbord which is more universal than the language compartments suggest. As one of the most ardent participants in this cosmopolitan feast, the Jew is divorced from the very parochial conditions which make a cultural definition possible.

Nor can one honestly assert that Jews are ethically distinct. Many apologists maintain that Jews possess moral virtues that other groups do not, and that group identity is defined by a set of commonly held ethical values. When pressed to be more specific, the defenders of this thesis usually resist. If they do make citations, they invoke the family unity of the Jewish home or the pursuit of education. Since neither of these values is uniquely Jewish, the moral definition collapses before the evidence. And since the ethical behavior of Jews is not noticeably superior to that of other groups, the thesis savors of a *hutspadik* pretense. Active Jewish liberalism may have many individual exponents; but it hardly characterizes the vast majority of contemporary Jews.

The attempt to equate Jewishness with a set of eminently respectable social values is an act of moral boorishness. It suggests, by implication, that these values (if they are defined as virtues) are absent from the behavior of non-Jews. Such an act of gracelessness is typical of the self-righteous. It reveals a kind of humorless arrogance (which is not uniquely Jewish).

Scholars who are desperate may end up by relegating Jewishness to the category of "mystery," or by peevishly asserting that "anyone is Jewish who says he is." But neither solution is satisfactory. The first romanticizes confusion; and the second ignores the involuntary character of Jewish identity.

An adequate definition of Jewish status must begin with an honest appraisal of how Jews identify each other. There is obviously an operative standard of inclusion and exclusion. It is neither theological nor racial nor cultural nor moral. If we look carefully we will see that it has less to do with personal behavior than with family connection.

Jewish status, like one's last name, is a matter of birth. As we are born into our nuclear family, so are we born into our Jewish condition. We may become theists or humanists, Zionists or anti-Zionists, Birchers or Marxists, devotees of Moses or lovers of Zen; but, as long as we and others are aware of our family tree, our Jewishness persists. Conventional Jewish mothers do not check the ideological commitments of their prospective sons-in-law; they want to know who the parents are. An antisemitic atheist from a Jewish womb is acceptable; a circumcised Hebrew-speaking American who believes in the truth of the Bible is not.

Conversion to Judaism has been historically rare, not only because of Christian persecution, but also because missionary prospects viewed Judaism as a kind of family affair. To become a Jew was not only to accept the discipline of the *Halakha* but also to assume the ancestry of Abraham. It was to sever one's familial connections and to pretend to be a child of another tribe. Without a pervasive sense of common forefathers, the religious bonds would have been insufficient to insure group unity. Even the blackest of Jewish blacks in Abyssinia and the most Tartarish of Jewish Tartars in the Crimea insisted on their physical descent from the patriarchs. Without that illusion, the legitimacy of their status would have been open to question.

Rabbinic Judaism affirmed this standard by declaring

that the offspring of a Jewish mother was irrevocably Jewish. No apostasy, no repudiation of hallowed beliefs, no mockery of community custom, could alter his identity. Jewishness came with the womb and expired only with death. New members might be adopted ('conversion' has an ideological non-Jewish overtone) into the group; but their acceptance and the acceptance of their children were never secure until the adoption was forgotten.

The outside world responded to this criterion by viewing Jewishness as an inherited condition. Disraeli may have been a devoted member of the Church of England, lauding the virtues of Protestant Christianity; but in the eyes of his public, he remained a Jew—albeit an Anglican one. Marx may have despised all forms of organized religion, branding them the opiate of the people; yet, in the view of both friend and foe, he was irresistibly Jewish—even though in an atheistic way. Womb identity was not an antisemitic invention; it was a venerable Jewish tradition, which both insiders and outsiders applied with consistency.

Now racial and familial identity must not be confused. The first implies (if we use the precise university definition) physical uniformity. The second only demands a sense of shared ancestors. Two people, of visibly different genetic makeup, may still share a common set of grandparents— or think they do. A family that started in Jerusalem might disperse itself throughout the world, intermarrying with wide varieties of racial types, and still retain the sense of closeness that common ancestry provides. The familial feeling would lie in genealogy—and not in physiology.

Even sharp cultural differences would not inhibit group intimacy. The Rothschilds became in each of their environments either impeccably English or impeccably French or impeccably German, without shedding the family loyalty that went beyond financial interest. Even the Sassoons, embracing Oriental and Occidental extremes, enjoyed a world-wide family unity. Racial, linguistic, and philosophic differences often surrender to the power of the *mishpakha* feeling.

Jews are no exception. As one of the oldest enduring extended families, they have spanned the world, participated in all its major cultures, savored all its vital religious ideologies, and simultaneously retained the group bond. Whether it be the pleasure of family roots or the pressure of external hostility, the cause of their togetherness has been independent of ethical value and cosmic belief.

An honest Judaism starts with this reality and builds on it. Instead of forcing Jews into ideological and cultural niches that do not fit, instead of defining Jewishness by universal moral values that most people never live up to, instead of foolishly trying to mold a people to meet the demands of a ruthless respectability, we ought to just relax with what we *really* are. We ought to good-humoredly confront the fact that if we insist on searching for a common set of theological notions or social values which describes all Jews, living or dead, we are condemned to futility. If we cannot accept membership in an international extended family united by feelings of shared ancestry and ties of common history, without the pretension of ethical distinction, we cannot accept our Jewishness. The propaganda of religious leaders and cultural secularists has refused to confront us with this truth.

A Jewish humanism uses this truth in assisting the modern Jew to be authentic. By affirming that Jewish identity is non-ideological and familial, it never forces the individual to compromise his integrity with the demand that he ought to believe what he doesn't believe. By insisting that Jewishness is independent of any kind of moral supremacy, it frees the person from pretending to be what he knows he is not. By equating group membership with family feeling instead of cultural uniqueness, it can confront the reality of our status without refusing to accept the nature of our assimilation. Jews and Jewishness may be both pro-social and anti-social, beautiful and ugly, wise and foolish. Jews may display behavior patterns which are sometimes admirable and sometimes disgusting, but perfectly normal and eminently human. Like all large families,

Jews have their fair share of saints and beasts as well as their fair quota of mystics and rationalists. Of course, none of these alternatives has anything to do with the state of being a Jew.

As a member of an old tribe with many memories the Jew is inevitably drawn to family anniversaries. These are called holidays and are as appropriate to the Jewish people as birthdays and wedding reminders are suitable to smaller clans. The realistic pleasures of Rosh Hashana, Hanukka, and Passover are usually familial, and have little or nothing to do with theological commitment. The old Haggadoth may be amusing leftovers of bygone societies, but Rosh Hashana survives as a meaningful affirmation of group identity. The fall holiday season more realistically celebrates the birth of the Jewish people than the birth of the world.

The Jewish calendar is a family calendar. While it ought to be enhanced and supplemented by celebrations that affirm our human identity, it gives us historic roots and invites us to enjoy our birthright without confusing it with questionable dogma and ludicrous pretension. Child education for Jewish humanists has two dimensions. One is information about man and his past which will enable the child to understand his intimate connection with all men; the other is an objective and scientific understanding of his Jewish family, which will provide him with suitable insight into his involuntary status as a Jew. Since the secular schools already provide most of the "human" information, it is the primary role of the temple school to afford the Jewish data. Of course, Jewish history must always be presented within the humanist assumption that human identity is primary and that Jews are as historically guilty of resisting this commitment as any other group. Teachers who view religious education as a defense and apology for historic Jewish beliefs and behavior are responsible for the hysterical character of current curriculum. Self-flattery is a symptom of self-hate; honesty is a sign of self-esteem.

If you ask reasonably: why bother with Jewish holidays

and Jewish history; why bother to perpetuate old "family" identities that have neither philosophic nor ethical uniqueness, the humanist answer emerges from unpleasant fact and realistic hope. The unpleasant fact is chronic antisemitism. It would be nice to live in a world where Jewish identity would not arouse the paranoiac fears of countless millions and would not be of great social importance to masses of people. But reality defies desire. Humanists who are Jews early discover that their humanism is of less significance to the public than their Jewishness. As long as external hostility exists (no matter how dramatically diminished), the Jewish family will exist. The only options open to the members of that family will be relaxed acceptance or futile resistance.

The realistic hope is a practical variation on a utopian dream of "one world." Since the greatest obstacle to human unity is the organized power of state nationalism, any existing group with strong internal loyalty which transcends state boundaries and unites people on an international scale is a welcome ally in a good cause. Whatever the allegiance, class, professional, or familial, if it enables people to feel a part of a society broader than their nation, it is a step in the right direction. Jews have been accused by their enemies of being both rootless and cosmopolitan. It is a hidden compliment that ought to be exploited.

Familial ties are never trivial. From the view of childhood conditioning, they make theological propositions and moral slogans look powerless. The question is: are they beneficial? If they become fearful obsessions with family survival, defensive apologies for group superiority, they do great harm. If, on the contrary, they sponsor a happy wedding of sentiment and individual integrity, they can be vehicles of immense social good.

Rationality

A former humanist confided to me that he had repented.

Most of his life he had believed that the best way to handle human problems was through the use of rational thinking. He had frowned on all forms of emotionalism and preferred to confront the realities of the world with cold objectivity. Mind over heart had been his credo and he pursued it relentlessly. The result of such consistency, he confessed, was a dramatic absence of any sense of personal fulfillment. Since the most important things in life cannot be trapped by logic, the purely rational approach to the solution of problems had proved a fiasco. He regretted that he had not seen the light sooner.

The accusation of this new "penitent" has become a familiar assault. A recent letter from a troubled rabbi denounces the pretensions of scientific humanists. The age of science, he asserts, has sponsored the two most devastating wars in human history, as well as Auschwitz. If rational thinking can produce results no better than these horrors, it has abdicated the right to be the arbiter of human decision. Perhaps the simple piety of the Hasidic saint with all its naïvete, irrational mystery, and intuitive commitment is morally superior to the sophisticated emptiness of logical solutions. The world may need less faith in reason and more faith in love.

A local Christian cleric pleaded that a philosophy of life that starts from a dispassionate view of people and nature can only produce human automatons, insensitive to emotional reality. Feeling, not logic, gives meaning to existence. The coldness of rational thinkers chills the operations of human society, and substitutes the superficial for the profound. Reason places a premium on the trivial events that can easily be described over those profound realities which can only be felt, but never described.

A university psychiatrist, who provided an able challenge at a recent debate, contended that most human reasoning is a defensive game. Rationality does not determine our decisions; it simply finds respectable excuses for the devious tyranny of certain feelings and desires we are afraid to reveal. Under the cool exterior of impeccable human logic lurk the irrational thoughts and visions of our childhood fears and fantasies. Most rationality is only rationalization. The social role of reason has rarely been the pursuit of truth. While reason pretends to reveal reality, it usually only succeeds in hiding it.

A writer of science textbooks mocked the value of reason for answering ultimate human questions. He pointed out that an empirical psychology can reveal the life goals that people *do* have; it cannot disclose the goals they *should* have. Rationality only measures efficiency. If one chooses to exterminate Jews, there is a reasonable way to go about doing it. And if one chooses to suffer, there is a rational program for effective masochism. Reason is morally neutral. Two businessmen who are well known in the Detroit commercial world for their unfailing success pooh-poohed the relevance of reason. Most decisions in life, they maintained, preclude rational investigation. There isn't enough time in any given day to adequately research the basic facts which are relevant to the most trivial of decisions. Most individuals who claim to be reasonable actually determine their actions by personal hunches, sudden intuitions, and a quick perusal of limited evidence. Life is too short for rationality. The pressure of decisions makes a mockery out of any extended claim to patient objectivity.

While the roster of objectors and objections to rationality continues indefinitely (for there is nothing more fashionable in current religious and literary circles than to denounce the adequacy of reason), it may be wise to pause and evaluate the familiar criticism we have just recalled.

The "Auschwitz argument," in particular, is one of the oldest and most durable in the anti-rationalist arsenal. Among Jews it carries an emotional charge which no other assault can equal. With a fanfare denunciation of the sins of science, rabbis gleefully thrust the challenge of the concentration camps into the faces of humanists. "If a people as scientific as the Germans have succumbed to such barbarism, then how can one praise the supreme value of empirical thinking?" The implication of the question is that in the twentieth century, whether we speak of Germany or America, we are living in the age of science.

But no view of the twentieth century is farther from reality. While it is true that empirical thinking dominates our research in the areas of physics and chemistry, it is false to assert that this procedure characterizes the ordinary approach to the study of human motivation and social behavior. The most sophisticated aeronautical engineer who can describe in detail the intricate operations of the jet plane motor, has only the most primitive conception of the nature of the human brain and nervous system. The most talented physicist whose discoveries have revolutionized our notions of interstellar space, has only the vaguest conception of the social causes of war, economic depression, and bigotry. The reasons for these deficiencies do not lie in their unwillingness to receive available information. The difficulty arises from the fact that very little scientific information is really available.

One may plead that human society does not easily lend itself to the controlled experiments which empiricism demands. But this observation only begs the question. It still remains a fact, that in the areas most intimately concerned with the values and behavior of men, scientific information has never replaced the inherited prejudices, intuitions, and tribal myths which control contemporary political behavior. In the crucial disciplines which purport to explain human nature, no age of science can even be detected. To combine a barely liberated empirical physics with a primitive sociology and to label this bizarre mixture as the natural expression of a scientific world is to win arguments by inventing straw men.

Perhaps our problem does not even start with the difficulty of investigating human behavior. Perhaps it begins with the terrified reluctance that most people express when someone sets out to probe and analyze their inmost thoughts and feelings. No one is emotionally threatened when the researcher intends to study the electrical operation of a computer. But when the investigator seeks to correlate the electrical system of the human brain with the emergence of certain ideas and feelings, he is accused of demeaning man. It is wiser to leave that realm of darkness in darkness, where ignorance can poetically be disguised by the clever bandying about of such informative terms as "soul," "personhood," and "I-Thou."

Auschwitz is no more an expression of the age of science than Albert Einstein is an expression of Jewish piety. Aggressive tribal nationalism is not the result of an insightful and sober analysis of the human psyche through empirical responsibility. It most likely is a self-righteous and self-pitying attempt to keep the reality of one's weakness and fears from conscious confrontation. Hitlerite hysteria, not a scientific psychology, produced it.

If the nature of science has been misconstrued, so has the role of feeling. The contention that the most important things in life are both indescribable and detected only through emotion leads only to confusion. Man's strongest feelings are not aroused by vague and nebulous notions which defy conception. Hostility, anger, and love are not responses to emptiness. If the object of their intensity cannot be described, it is hardly because it is indescribable. It is more likely because its concept is too frightening, too threatening, or socially too embarrassing to verbalize. A perfect parallel presents itself in ancient Jewish practice. Graven images of Yahveh were not prohibited because Yahveh had no face. They were forbidden because the face of Yahveh was so terrifyingly radiant that to gaze on it was to die.

The human unconscious is filled with all kinds of objects like the imagined faces of Yahveh. They are scarily specific or benevolently detailed, and like father and mother awaken the strongest emotions. On the conscious level we feel the pleasure or pain of the feeling but have conveniently forgotten the object. In fact, we prefer only dim recollections. The less specific and the less describable we pretend the source of our feelings to be, the less likely are we to truly confront it. And then we crown our deception by pleading mystery.

There are presently many events in the universe which defy easy description. Their status is not due to some inherent inconceivability; it is rather due to the primitive character of our language, which is not sufficiently precise. The task of the sensible philosopher is not to plead an incurable verbal helplessness (a rationalization for fear), but to improve and refine our language by the creation of new words. To substitute worship for analysis is to inhibit self-insight.

The university psychiatrist is correct in his assertion that most "rationality" is only rationalization. While the fantasy ideas and opinions that populate our subconscious actually control our emotional responses and determine our personal behavior, we exhaust ourselves with naïve self-deception in justifying their consequences. Intellectual conversation so often turns sour and meaningless, simply because it is the most guilty of this pretension.

But to assert that human behavior is chiefly under the control of irrational ideas, and that most so-called rational conversation is pure sham, in no way invalidates the value of reason. It only implies that it is harder to be reasonable than we imagined. Logic without self-insight is a child's game that condemns us to repeat the suffering of the past, but rational thinking *means,* first of all, self-knowledge. Unless we are aware of the true nature of our subconscious visions, we cannot change them. The goal of life is not to wallow in self-pity and to meekly accept the tyranny of irrational ideas. It is to risk the discovery of these irrational ideas, and, if possible, transform them.

The rational goal of life is happiness, the previously-cited science writer notwithstanding. While it is possible to plan a world in which pain will be maximized and pleasure will be minimized, the reverse seems more reasonable, given the ordinary meaning of the word. To pursue pain and self-destruction with logical efficiency may be rational in the narrow sense of effectiveness. It is irrational in the broader sense of conforming to universal desires. Although the rational categories of truth and falsity apply only to ideas and cannot be attached to desires, the pursuit of suffering for the sake of suffering is unreasonable by association. It defies what rational thinking has historically been used to achieve.

However, to be reasonable is an aspiration, not a reality. It is not only challenged by fantasies deep-rooted in the human psyche; it is also frustrated by the urgent demands of time. If daily decisions must be made quickly, as our businessmen confirm, life is too short for rationality. Intuitive hunches and risky plunges are far more characteristic of the chaos of normal living.

However, many intuitions are often more than they seem. They may be the inarticulate common-sensical observations of years of practical experience (for example, quick-thinking successful entrepreneurs with no formal education) or they may be sensible evaluations for which the evidence has long since been forgotten. They do not defy rational thinking; they are simply primitive expressions of it.

Sometimes, doing lengthy, detailed, and painstaking research is a sign of being irrational. If the purpose of study is to control action, study which prevents action is absurd. When our happiness at a given moment depends upon our willingness to make quick and risky decisions, delay, for the sake of analysis, is unreasonable. Rationality does not imply an exhaustive survey of all facts relevant to a particular problem. (If we had to do that, we would never take any action.) It rather implies the desire to confront as much of the available evidence in the time limits of a given situation. Only the gods claimed to be omniscient; human beings have to settle for intelligence.

The sensitive rational humanist sticks to reason, not because he is an enthusiastic devotee of logical order. He just isn't aware of any alternative procedure that is better suited to reduce human suffering and enhance human pleasure. He does not presume, in some pollyannish fashion, that it is easy to be reasonable. He understands the perils of self-deception and arid justification, while affirming the riskiness of all decisions. Although he knows that he does not yet live in an age of science, he hopes that man's self-understanding will grow. If he rejects the notion that he must choose between being either "cold" or "warm," he does so with the knowledge that passion and objectivity are not mutually exclusive. They are indispensable partners in the work of human happiness.

Community

In a recent conversation with a stranger, I described the program of our congregation. I emphasized that one of our major functions was to provide an atmosphere of free inquiry in which major ethical problems could be discussed. The stimulus of mutual challenge was intended to enable each individual member to achieve his own moral conclusions.

The stranger listened and laughed. He replied that what our society needed was not another ethical discussion society; talk was cheap and useless. What was required was action. In a world of war, prejudice, and economic poverty, the willingness to respond to the moral challenge by taking fearless and decisive action is the basic necessity. Ethical discussion is a poor substitute for ethical action. Organized verbalizing will never solve any problems; nor is group therapy an adequate replacement for social commitment. He described his own personal involvement in the work of civil rights groups and his admiration for those brave souls who preferred the risk of doing to the doubtful benefits of "agonizing" appraisal.

On a first hearing, the stranger's point seemed very telling. Undoubtedly, there are countless people in our society, including our own vulnerable selves, who talk a great deal about our moral commitments and never do anything to implement our conclusions. The rosters of all discussion groups are filled with hundreds of "cocktail heroes" who declare their liberal attachment to social reform in the privacy of their living room and simultaneously refuse to open their mouths in the public arena. Hypocrisy is a rather common human failing.

But the stranger was saying something more. He implied that discussion was valueless, that talking provided no positive benefits. A hidden premise supported his argument and pervaded his whole approach. If people fail to act decisively and courageously in the face of ethical challenge, it is not because they are ignorant of what is right and wrong; it is because they are either too "chicken" to plunge or too blasé to care. Inability to respond is not the result of honest confusion; it is a function of chronic cowardice.

The stranger's analysis is not unique. Many philosophers have assumed that the primary ethical problems are either fear or malice. When the prophet Amos uttered the famous line, "pursue good and not evil," he had no doubts as to what was good and what was evil. The moral issue, as he saw it, was not that his audience was uninformed; it lay in the perverse unwillingness of the people to do what they really knew they ought to do. For Amos the call of justice was never confusing. Sacrificing animals and lending money on interest were obviously wrong. If the citizens of Israel refused to do what their historic conscience told them to do, they deserved the punishment he predicted. The function of the righteous man is to proclaim the ethical truth. Since there is nothing to be learned from the wicked, open discussion is a wasteful luxury.

The well-intentioned fanatic is a fixture of every society. His credentials are the absolute certainty he feels on all ethical issues. His agony may be profound; yet it is never associated with his own moral confusion. It is rather the pain he feels for the blindness of his enemies. Like Jesus he may refuse to hate the opposition; but he confers a gift that makes hatred preferable—the sickening touch of patronizing pity. He may graciously assume the "humble" pose of admitting that he often fails to *do* what is right, but he will never suggest that he does not *know* what is right.

Next to cynicism and self-pity, no human quality is more unattractive, or more dangerous, than self-righteousness. To assume that one's personal intuitions are the ultimate arbiters of ethical issues is to make social conditioning an infallible judge. It is to reduce every moral question to the setting of an American western, where the "good guys" never talk to the "bad guys"—they just shoot them.

A common-sensical and practical ethics frowns on absolute certainty. Its refusal to allow either fanaticism or self-righteousness arises from no weakness of the heart or mind; it is the result of three rather obvious conditions.

1. The value of any activity is determined by its consequences—by its effect on the welfare of oneself and other people. Since morality is a function of human happiness, no action is intrinsically right or wrong. Whatever behavior in a given situation appears most conducive to promoting human fulfillment is the proper one to choose. Artificial birth control may be wrong in a situation of diminishing fertility; it may be right in the midst of a population explosion. One-man dictatorship may be proper in the wake of flood and earthquake disaster; it may be thoroughly improper in the context of a secure and prosperous community. Certain general rules, like truth-telling and non-violence, may emerge from the test of human experience; but "white lies" and defensive wars announce the exceptions. Intelligent ethical judgments are the products of continual testing and discussion. A moral decision of today may be refuted by the evidence of tomorrow.

2. Happiness is a delicate balance of different experiences. Love, creativity, power, recognition, and security are all essential to the harmony. No one value defines fulfillment. The talented economist who settles for a minor civil service job in order to find total security needs more than security. The black protester who drives himself to achieve equality with his white neighbors needs more than social recognition. Many a "liberal" parent has faced the dilemma of choosing between the value of an integrated urban

society and the opportunity of a superior suburban school system. Do the social advantages of exposure to many kinds of people outweigh the informational benefits of expert academic instruction? It is easy to forget the balance and overemphasize one ingredient. The puritan, the pacifist, and the anarchist are perfect examples of what an obsession with a single value can do. While their ethical actions may be courageously hard, their ethical judgments are naïvely simple.

3. The "public" and the "public good" are linguistic fictions; they make what is obviously plural appear to be singular. Society is, in reality, a mad collection of countless individuals, each with a unique formula for personal salvation. To jibe and to reconcile the desires and needs of three billion souls is a task not to be achieved by merely "listening to conscience." Without the continuing disclosures of the psychological and social sciences no intelligent decision can be made. The political and economic problems of modern urban culture cannot be solved by the quick intuitions of peasant prophets. The current dilemmas of civil rights and automation are not the result of the citizens' unwillingness to *do* what is right; they largely thrive on the inability of even the most intelligent to *know* what is right.

Common-sense ethics functions with the important premise that moral certainty is impossible. It welcomes experimentation and assumes that goodwill and valuable advice are not the exclusive possessions of "my side." While it freely admits that morality means moral action, it acknowledges that the study of evidence and the challenge of discussion are indispensable to intelligent decision. Talking may be cheap; but it is very necessary.

Pleasure

Some indignant Jew called me an *apikoros* the other day. He thought it was an insulting epithet, designating the rejection of all that was essentially Jewish. Little did he realize that for me it was a kind of unintended compliment. The word *apikoros,* the traditional Talmudic label for theological skeptics, is the rabbinic corruption of the Greek name *Epicurus.* And Epicurus is one of my favorite philosophers.

Epicurus inspired a particular horror in the rabbinic mind because he unequivocally affirmed that the greatest good was human pleasure. "For we recognize pleasure," he said, "as the first good innate in us, and from pleasure we begin every act of choice and avoidance, and to pleasure we return again, using the feeling as a standard by which we judge every good." To ignore divine will as the ultimate standard of virtue seemed especially offensive and subverted the traditional notions of duty and sacrificial service. The rabbis were perfectly amenable to accepting pleasure as a consequence of right action as long as it was never presumed to be the criterion of morality.

Jewish opposition to Epicurus was not unique. Christian theologians found in this humanistic Greek the source of all evil and the devilish cleverness of Satan. From Augustus to Pius X few philosophers have received more frequent church denunciations. Modern day hedonists, conditioned by the historic opposition, prefer to use such euphemisms as "happiness" or "the satisfaction of desire" in order to avoid the dread accusation of "pursuing pleasure." The last phrase carried, in our Christian civilization, a dirty connotation. If one chooses to endorse its meaning as an ultimate value, he must be prepared to apologize for his choice.

From the record of religious opposition, one would imagine that "the ogre" in question was a grotesque and venereal glutton whose debauched body decayed from overindulgence. Yet no conception is further from the truth. Epicurus was a successful fourth century Athenian teacher. His manner of living was both abstemious and ascetic, and was dominated by immense self-control. Although he is justly called the father of hedonism, his interests in sex and food were minimal. The value he preferred above all others is nothing more ecstatic than the pleasure of friendship.

However, the monastic quality of his life has not deterred his detractors. If they no longer attack his personal habits, they still assault his premises and declare them dangerous. The following six objections summarize the modern opposition.

1. It may be true that man instinctively does pursue pleasure. But this fact will not imply that man *should* pursue pleasure. One cannot deduce an *ought* from an *is*. Morality may simply require that man resist his nature rather than indulge it.

2. Even psychology à la Sigmund Freud asserts that man does in fact, concern himself with more than pleasure. The erotic desires of childhood must confront the demands of personal survival. If an individual desires to live, he must come to terms with the social norms of his environment. The reality principle is as significant in man as the pleasure principle.

3. We live in a post-Christian age. The pursuit of pleasure already dominates our decision and behavior. Yet increased anxiety, and not fulfillment, seems to be the consequence. Indulgence in pleasure appears to aggravate our insecurity.

4. Since pleasure is personal and subjective, altruism and social concern are incompatible with hedonism. The fabric of human society, which is woven by mutual sacrifice and benevolence, falls apart when selfishness becomes respectable. Hedonism is an antisocial doctrine.

5. Pleasure is vegetative. The goal of life must certainly be more significant than the mere relief of tension. To justify sex passion and food lust is nice and necessary but never enough.

6. If a man finds murder pleasant, then the logic of hedonism dictates, in the absence of "law" enforcement, that he should freely kill. The violent antisocial desires of the human psyche need only plead pleasant satisfaction and they will be justified.

The answers to these objections rest on the strong conviction that most people fail to distinguish between a gross philosophy of pleasure and an enlightened hedonism.

1. Historic Christianity reveals in its doctrine of man a sadistic tendency. God presumably makes demands on the human race which he knows its essential nature resists. Ethical demand promotes only the pain of human frustration. Since man is not, by the makeup of his desire, able to do what he is asked to do, God "graciously" forgives man for not being able to execute the impossible. There is a malicious humor in a deity who designs man with a built-in "disobedience" and then blames him for not being able to transcend it.

Rabbinic Judaism does not do much better. The demands of the Torah are so numerous and the *halachic* discipline so severe, that Jews are always bound to end up a "stiff-necked people." In the end only the "merits of the fathers" redeems them. If God had not loved Abraham and made a promise to him, the Jews would have no vicarious out.

There is something both perverse and amusing about a philosophy of life that derives its ideals from what man cannot possibly become. To demand of man behavior unrelated to his basic desires is to provide no motivation for ethical action. It is to invest in a game in which all the players are destined to fail. If the pursuit of pleasure, whatever its evolutionary origins, is the heart of the human psyche, morality begins with this fact. If the game of ethics is indifferent to what a man desires most, then why should he bother to play the game? There is so much idiotic cruelty in the world that morality might compassionately avoid adding to it.

2. Although Freud speaks of both a pleasure principle and a reality principle as governing factors in human behavior, the two forces are substantially one. After all, the reality principle derives from the need of man to adjust his behavior to the demands of his social environment. The critical persuader which induces the human child to socialize his actions is the pain of punishment, and the flight from pain is only the reverse side of the pursuit of pleasure.

Man is by nature and need a social animal. Exclusion from human fellowship subverts his survival. The prospect of death is less terrifying than the possibility of lonely isolation. The very will to live arises from the stimulus of human intercourse. The pleasures of indiscriminate violence are outweighed by the pain of social rejection.

3. To object to the pursuit of pleasure because it yields anxiety is to ironically denounce hedonism because it isn't pleasurable. Obviously, a so-called pleasure which is accompanied by the pain of relentless anxiety is, in reality, no pleasure at all. It may be nothing more than a mask for fear.

In fact, our modern culture is replete with pseudo-pleasures, the appearance of which is respectably satisfying. But beneath the veneer of ecstasy and joy, lies the pain of agonizing fear. The neurosis of pseudo-pleasure is a desperate attempt to deny pain by calling it pleasant. The surface tranquility is only a clumsy disguise.

Is the penchant for personal privacy in our bourgeois culture a legitimate attempt to "get away from it all," or is it really an expression of our fear of exposure, the terror of others seeing what we really are? Is the present obsession with sexual activity an honest revelation of our erotic needs, or is it basically a frantic cry of human helplessness in the anonymous urban jungle of modern technology? Can the users of narcotics be designated rational joy seekers, or are they self-destructive self-haters who confuse masochism with ecstasy? Are the defenders of tradition serenely indulging the pleasure of group immortality, or are they militantly acting out their fear of a continually changing world?

The test of genuine happiness is the absence of desperation. Most self-confessed pleasure seekers would never pass this test.

4. It is commonplace to accuse people who pursue personal pleasure of selfishness. If 'selfishness' describes a man who consciously or unconsciously always seeks to insure his personal survival, then hedonism is often opposed to it. There are many situations where long-run

pleasure and personal survival are incompatible.

The dynamic of altruism, in the absence of the pressures of government and public opinion, need not be in some coldly abstract principle called 'duty'. (Even the church and synagogue recognized the inadequacy of such an appeal. They provided the rewards of paradise and the fires of the pit as an 'extra' inducement.) The human source of brotherhood lies in a universal capacity of man's nervous system. It is the ability to empathize.

Empathy is the ability not only to see another person's pain but also to feel it—not only to perceive another's happiness but also to identify with it. In the empathic situation 'your pain' becomes 'my pain' and 'your pleasure' becomes 'my pleasure'. Golden rules are meaningless directives when divorced from the flesh and blood reality of transferred emotions. The ethically sensitive person is not the rigid man of duty; he is the intelligent hedonist who understands that the suffering of others cannot be separated from *his* pain; nor can the needs of others be cut away from *his* needs. Outside of common peril and social coercion, empathy is the emotional glue of human cooperation.

5. To maintain that pleasure is vegetative is to ignore the fact that certain pleasures are preferable to others. If joys can be measured by intensity, they can also be distinguished by quality. Many pleasures provide a quick release of tension but carry with them the anxiety of dependence and insecurity. Others feature a slower relief but confer the thrill of independence and power.

Happiness dependent on the possession of physical objects or particular persons is always tenuous. The anxiety of possible loss creates a sense of fearful dependence and gives life a certain tone of clutching and painful desperation. But human happiness that depends on the ideas and talents of the man himself elevates self-esteem and provides daily living with the security of alternatives. If one knows that he has the power to create objects and services useful to himself and others, greediness is unnecessary. In fact the sign of his pleasurable security is that he can share freely. His gifts to others are never sacrificial offerings; they are delightful expressions of human power.

The pleasure of self-control is equally a manifestation of this need for strength. Countless dieters, despite all the agonies of initial deprivation, find that the power to dismiss unnecessary food pleasurably surpasses the clutchiness of compulsive tasting. Ecstasies that remind us of our weakness and dependence turn empty quickly.

6. There is no doubt that many human drives are antisocial. If they are indulged in the 'real' world of business and politics, community survival is threatened. If they are practiced in a substitute world of the theater and sports, they become socially harmless and are respectably drained of their venom.

Given our primate past, there is lots of violence in our genes. Given the technical triumph of human civilization, there is obviously an equally strong disposition to social cooperation. Since we cannot indulge both pleasures in the 'real' world, we must choose between them. Commonsensical observation would indicate that the creative pleasures of social intercourse outweigh the long-run possibilities of violence.

A sensible society expresses its choice by understanding our underlying violence. It encourages competitive spectator sports, a theater filled with stories of rape and murder, and a gory cinema. It even smears the fairy tales of children with gallons of imaginary blood. The peace program is for real life.

An enlightened Epicurean is neither selfish, vegetative, nor pollyannish. He is the most rational and compassionate of moralists. He finds in happiness a favorable balance of pleasure over pain and declares it to be the best of all possible goals.

Universalism

Should Jews marry only Jews?

Most Jews think that they should. Even the most sophisticated prefer the perils of atheism to the trauma of mixed weddings. The prospect that their children will be doing their reproducing with Gentiles arouses the deepest aversion that their unconscious can conjure up. Notorious liberals who are big on brotherhood, legalized marijuana, and female liberation, often turn hysterical when they learn that their Jewish sons intend to cohabit in a legal way with non-Jewish girls. Infamous Jewish antisemites, who are turned off by all forms of organized religion and who find Jewish culture depressing, are known to become violent when their daughters announce their intentions to marry Gentile boys.

Why?

Why this almost inexplicable overreaction to decent love?

The answer is important, because no issue in American Jewish life is as explosive as the question of intermarriage. Even the Reform rabbinate, the so-called paragons of religious liberalism, are deeply divided on the issue. One witnesses the ironic spectacle of radical egalitarians and libertarians turning into fanatic inquisitors, eager to expel erring rabbis from the rabbinic fold for the unspeakable sin of officiating at mixed marriages.

The reason for this behavior is no mystery. Tribal loyalty is an old and respectable human attachment. Although it is not uniquely Jewish, it has been aggravated among Jews by centuries of exile and homelessness. Jews have had to make a special effort to survive as a group. Without the dramatic difference of their rituals, food, language, and dress from the customs of their neighbors, they would have long since been assimilated.

Our ancestors had to work very hard to maintain these differences. As a result, we feel very guilty when we give them up. Even when we no longer believe in the viability of traditional customs, even when the tyranny of outmoded practices violates our individual integrity, we often consent to continue them. The guilt of repudiating what so many of our ancestors died to preserve is too much for us to bear.

The most effective technique for group survival in an alien

environment was social segregation and compulsory inbreeding. The ban on intermarriage followed logically from the overwhelming desire to preserve Jewish identity. People who reproduce together stay together. As a technique for the maintenance of dispersed minorities, this prohibition was both universal and familiar. The Aryan conquerors of India used it well when they devised the caste system. And English colonials found it useful in the preservation of Anglo-Saxon identity in the most threatening environments.

The Jewish ban on intermarriage dates from the sixth century B.C. When the Jewish aristocracy was taken by the Chaldeans to a Babylonian exile, they found themselves a small minority in a sea of Semitic strangers. Too snobbish to assimilate and too affluent to forego the new luxuries of Babylon for the rural poverty of Judea, they turned to rigid inbreeding as a way of enjoying the best of two worlds. Under the leadership of fanatic priests, they elevated their new custom into divine law. The Zadokite priests inserted this prohibition into the text of the Torah which they were writing and gave it a divine aura.

When some of the Babylonian Jews returned to Jerusalem in the fifth century, they brought with them both the Torah and the ban. Their charismatic leader Ezra forced the native Jews to accept the authority of the Torah and to divorce their non-Jewish wives. Although many protested, the will of Ezra prevailed. From that traumatic moment on, inbreeding became a sacred and uncontested norm of Jewish orthodoxy.

In contemporary America the prohibition against outmarriage is of crucial importance to Jewish survivalists. With the rapid disappearance of most uniquely Jewish forms of behavior and with the quick assimilation of Jews to the Anglo-Saxon culture of urban America, the only barrier that stands between group identity and the ethnic melting pot is segregated reproduction.

Because of the contemporary 'crisis' in white America, where all European ethnic groups are quickly merging into one American nationality (and where the black nationality remains conspicuously distinct), a new militancy has emerged. Among Jews it manifests itself in verbal affirmations of the value of a pluralistic American society in which many national cultures can thrive side by side (although the Yiddish linguistic uniqueness on which such a difference could reasonably stand has long since been rejected). It also reveals itself in an atavistic, desperate espousal of the virtue of 'marrying your own kind'.

Since group survival for the sake of group survival is no longer publicly respectable, Jewish professionals are driven to find 'noble' reasons for this parochialism. Jews and Gentiles are annually feted with a variety of books which make the old claim that without Jewish exclusiveness mankind would enjoy less brotherhood, justice, and intellectual greatness. A world without Jews, they claim, would almost be a world not worth having.

Threatened minorities do not survive unconsciously (like the Russians and the Chinese). They often survive only by becoming obsessed with the problem of their own survival. Everything in Jewish life today is seen from the perspective of group identity. For many Jewish professionals, synagogue social action, experimental services, and the updating of Jewish philosophy are not avenues for individual fulfillment. They are gimmicks for involving Jews in Jewish institutions. Their value is a function of their ability to promote Jewish identity.

Even most liberal rabbis who consent to officiate at mixed marriages are apologetic about their activity. They are often embarrassed by their natural empathy for two individuals who love each other and feel impelled to justify their action in group terms. They, therefore, maintain that if they refuse to officiate the couple will choose to get married in a purely secular or Christian setting and that any opportunity to keep the erring lovers in the Jewish fold will be lost. Intermarriage is bad, they admit; but losing a Jew for good is worse.

So great is the guilt of deserting the group that the moral worth of individual happiness and personal love is lost in timid and defensive arguments about group survival.

Irrational comparisons between the European holocaust and assimilation crop up in the reasoning of self-proclaimed liberal theologians. How can we complete the work of Hitler, they cry, by allowing the Jew to disappear? As though the physical extermination of individuals was equivalent to the opportunity of individuals to freely choose their own identities.

The issue is clear.

If you believe that the most important Jewish enterprise is the promotion of Jewish identity, then the ban on inter-marriage is perfectly rational as a means to that end. If the primary purpose of the individual Jew is to affirm the sacrifices of his ancestors and to subordinate his personal happiness to the survival of the ethnic family into which he was born, then denouncing the immorality of outmarriage is a logical consequence.

If, on the other hand, the primary goal of the individual Jew is to secure his own happiness and fulfillment, then the ban on intermarriage is an unethical interference. If the purpose of a group, whether ethnic, religious, or profes-sional, is to serve the welfare of its individual members (and not to use its members to guarantee its own survival), then the refusal of rabbis to place personal love above Jewish identity is a form of moral negligence.

Certainly, it would be wrong to pretend that traditional Jewish ethics are neutral toward these options. As a group-oriented conventional morality, they make the same de-mand on the individual that the morality of any threatened minority makes. The rabbis of old would find an individual-istic ethic abhorrent and subversive of the divine will.

A humanistic morality, which affirms the ultimate value of the individual, has never been a part of any national religion, least of all the Jewish variety.

But that historic truth is irrelevant to a decent choice. Since ancestors *can* be wrong, and since it is possible to affirm that reality without guilt, Jewish humanists have the freedom to change what their conscience, their reason, and their empathy demand be changed.

A consistent humanist maintains the right of an individual to pursue his own happiness in the way that his personal needs and temperament require, so long as he does not interfere with the right of other individuals to do the same. He maintains the right of any Jew to marry whomever he chooses and is happy to assist him in exercising this choice. Since he recognizes the value of personal love to human happiness, he welcomes the fact that two people love each other, regardless of their religious and ethnic backgrounds. And since there is no empirical evidence to indicate that in-group marriages are more meaningful or more beneficial to children than inter-group marriages, he prefers to allow each marriage to rest on its own merits. The most important factors in the success of the family institution are independent of inherited religious labels.

A courageous and morally sensitive Jewish humanism must proclaim what no other Jewish group is presently willing to proclaim. It must declare that intermarriage is neither bad nor good. It must declare that every marriage should be judged by its personal consequences, by the degree of personal happiness and fulfillment it provides.

V
THE REAL HISTORY OF THE JEWS

Judaism

At an evening discussion recently, a hostile critic of Humanistic Judaism vehemently expressed his objections to our inclusion of the word *Judaism* to describe our organization. "I have no objection," he said, "to your calling yourself Jewish. After all, there is something we call Jewish culture and you do indulge in that. But there is a basic distinction between Jewishness and Judaism. Jewishness is an attachment to the habits of ethnic identity; Judaism is a religious philosophy of life. If you wish to call your viewpoint Jewish Humanism—fine and dandy! But Humanistic Judaism—never!"

As my critic proceeded to expound his argument more fully, I discerned, despite his increasing hostility, that he was making a valid point. There is indeed a clear distinction between Jewishness and Judaism. While religious customs and ceremonies may very well be a part of a national culture, and while certain theological doctrines may be indistinguishable from ethnic loyalty, it is certainly not true that viable national mores require either holy days or a doctrine about the universe. Secular Israelis may easily gorge themselves on the delicacies of a unique cultural buffet without being forced at any time to taste a theory about the religious significance of being Jewish.

Nevertheless, however perceptive my critic was in noting a value difference, he was certainly mistaken in maintaining that the commitment of Humanistic Jews was to Jewishness and not to Judaism. He was right in assuming that we were interested in the aesthetic achievements and creative possibilities of Jewish culture; he was wrong in concluding that this was the limit of our Jewish concern.

In fact, to assume that we are dedicated to the survival of a vital Jewish culture outside the state of Israel is to question our sanity and to accuse us of empirical irresponsibility to the facts of diaspora living. For only the cliché mongers of our community would be so bold as to affirm that any Jewish society, organization, or congregation in our American milieu has the power to outvote the massive conformity of all ethnic minorities to the requirements of a secular Anglo-Saxonism. Too many Jewish groups and movements suffer from the grandiose delusion that a viable diaspora culture is possible and choose, through either fear or blindness, to ignore the assimilationist behavior patterns of their own constituents. The harsh reality of Jewish culture in America is a dilettante procedure—the periodic indulgence of ceremonial and linguistic tidbits on nostalgic occasions. Neither the aggressiveness of day schools nor the self-mesmerizing propaganda of the rabbinic leadership has the social power to alter this reality.

The death in the Western world of other than vestigial Jewish culture is the result of two factors. First, the Jews in a bourgeois setting prefer, for obvious reasons, to identify with the social patterns that confer maximum social prestige. While in certain circles it is now fashionable to be a Jew, it has never been fashionable to be Jewish. (A few cultural crumbs may survive as just the right touch of exotic charm.) Secondly, the heart of any unique culture is a unique language. Zionists, French Canadians, and the

Latvian League are witnesses by their sweat and sacrifice to that truth. Jewish culture without the living presence of spoken Hebrew or Yiddish is mere pretense. Fry English in *schmaltz* if you will, it will do no good. You cannot eliminate the historical memories of a thousand years of separate linguistic development. Nor will a hundred hours per Jew per week of intense Hebrew training restore the language to American Jewish speech. Only a tongue that exceeds English in local prestige has a chance to survive. The humiliation of secular Jewish institutions that have struggled in vain to preserve even a semblance of Jewish cultural identity is evidenced by their increasing surrender to programs of Jewish studies in English. Imagine the Hong Kong British colony doing Shakespeare in Chinese!

Under these circumstances it would be foolish for any Jewish institution in America to define its Jewish commitments in terms of a distinctive Jewish culture. To pursue a goal which the evidence indicates is neither feasible nor achievable is immoral masochism. And much of Jewish institutional life is precisely that. For a realistic appraisal of the Jewish condition appears much too threatening.

In truth, certain outstanding facts about the nature of Jewish identity in America are available to any observer who dares to be objective.

1. The Jew in America both prefers and is conditioned to prefer the full-time consuming procedures of English-speaking culture. The Reconstructionist or secularist proposal that Jewish culture be preserved as a vital secondary alternative is founded on illusion. A secondary culture requires a secondary language; and a secondary language in middle-class society is viable only if it is prestigious (e.g. English in India, French in Lebanon). It is highly unlikely that more than a minute percentage of the Jewish community will acquire and retain fluency in Hebrew to the point where it can be used as an effective domestic language. Given the existing assimiliation in both food and dress, a realistic appraisal of a distinctive Jewish culture survival must indicate that the unique items of Jewishness

will remain as occasional affectations (now and then a Hebrew song, now and then an Israeli dance, now and then a food nostalgia).

2. Judaism, historically, was not only a religious philosophy *of* the Jewish people; it was a doctrine *about* the Jewish people (just as Christianity is not only the teaching *of* Jesus, but a teaching *about* Jesus). Traditionally, the rabbinic teachers viewed their people as custodians of a special divine revelation, which would be indicated to the world at the coming of the Messiah. As the upholders of a Levitical monotheism, they would demonstrate by their devotion and sacrifice the irresistible truth of their faith. However, this vision of the Jewish people is today a pure anachronism. While it may have accurately described the Jewish self-image in medieval Poland, it has absolutely no effective relationship to the self-view of Jews in contemporary America. Outside of pulpit rabbinics, it would be hard to find any Jew in bourgeois America who would voluntarily articulate this concept of religious mission as his own belief. In an age when the great majority of young Jewish people are, for good reason, vastly disinterested in the historic theology of Judaism, and when the scientific spirit has challenged the meaningfulness of the old religious language, the sense of a monotheistic mission is somewhat ludicrous. Not only is a functioning Jewish culture outside Israel not feasible, but also the old Judaism with its special view of the Jewish role is equally inoperable. The Jewish people in real life have nothing at all to do with the Jewish people portrayed in the official propaganda.

3. Neither is Jewish identity in the contemporary Western world a function of culture, race, or belief. It is a matter of birth and historical memory. On the negative side it is sustained by the persistent undercurrents of antisemitism and the nostalgic ties of family loyalty. On the positive side it is promoted by pride in Jewish achievement both present and past. Jewish identity among the new generation of American college students is sometimes bewilderingly

unclassifiable. It includes neither any sense of cultural difference nor any awareness of distinctive belief. Even "looking Jewish" is no longer its proper reference, for the old game of identifying the Jews in a crowd is becoming increasingly more difficult. Simply put, Jews have evolved in the contemporary world as a social caste, which is not racially identifiable, but in which membership is determined by birth or adoption. This caste, like all such social units, is characterized by intermarriage and mutual socializing and by a strong sense of shared fate. The intensity of "feeling Jewish" is not a function of cultural exposure or theological belief. It is related to the individual's awareness of his situation in society and in history.

4. The Jew in the Western world occupies a somewhat unique position. In the American environment he has become the most urbanized and educationally sophisticated of all caste groups. His image has altered from that of a bizarre outsider to that of a slightly "different" intellectual elite. Even the epithets of the antisemite which denounce his internationalism and rationalism ironically turn into the highest compliments a humanist can receive. The reality of Jewish life in the last third of the twentieth century is that the Jew has become, whether consciously or unconsciously, the vanguard of a humanistic outlook on life. In fact, the contemporary Jew is much more the "missionary" of a rational humanism than he is the promoter of a Biblical monotheism. The situation and role of modern Jewry is the very opposite of what traditional dogmatics assert. And a Judaism that desires to be more than merely pretty phrases without substance must come to terms with both of them.

If, then, we wish to understand Humanistic Judaism, its special approach lies in the fact that no empirical religion can ignore or turn its back on what it *is*. It is indeed immoral to foist on the public a sense of Jewish mission and intention that Jews by deed and persistent behavior refuse to assume. An "honest" Judaism views the present religious role of the Jewish group in a way that is consistent with their own self-image and achievement.

Humanistic Judaism is distinct, to some degree, from Jewish humanism in that it transcends the dubious relevance of a distinctive Jewish culture outside of the occasional aesthetic and ceremonial re-enforcement and concentrates on a view of the religious role of the contemporary Jew. Its radical readjustment lies in its description of this role. It does not see the Jew as the realistic promoter of theology; it rather views him by virtue of his caste identity, social situation, and historical memories, as an ideal advocate of humanism.

The task of a Humanistic Judaism is to educate the Jew to understand his *real* condition. It can do this by allowing him to explore and analyze his history in an empirically respectable way and by helping him to comprehend how he got where he is. It must also enable him to realistically assess the social situation in which he finds himself and discover how he can best use his given Jewish identity to promote the welfare of himself and all men.

Internationalism

Thousands and thousands of Jews have no public voice.

They are alienated from the official statements of official institutions. The leaders of Orthodoxy, Conservatism, Reform, Secularism, and Zionism do not articulate their beliefs. Since they are not prepared to give up their Jewish identity, they are condemned to being represented by public statements that have nothing at all to do with their convictions.

Why are they alienated?

Many are turned off by the mumbo jumbo of theology. They come to the synagogue to receive some kind of meaningful guidance for their daily lives and find themselves involved in a world of theistic fantasy where the rules of the game have nothing at all to do with real life. Too rational to accept romantic nostalgia as an adequate substitute and too honest to stomach hyprocrisy, they enter the limbo of malcontents who have no Jewish alternatives. Unlike their friends who have chosen compromise, they are not burdened by family guilt or peer pressure. Unlike their friends who have chosen "to leave," they find Unitarianism and Ethical Culture deficient in Jewishness.

Many are repelled by the open hypocrisy. There seems to be no correlation between what Jews say they believe and what they do. The Torah is exalted as the ultimate book of wisdom and no one reads it. The Talmud is praised as a source of great ethical insight and no one consults it. Prayer is announced as an essential human discipline and everyone ignores it. Judaism appears to be an immense pretension, a behavioral lie. For some Jews this game of illusions is necessary for Jewish survival. For others less willing to subordinate their personal integrity to a doubtful strategy, the inconsistency is insufferable.

Many are alienated by an absence of real experiment. In established institutions, whether conservative, reform, or reconstructionist, change has been trivial—a jazz service here, a cinema service there, but no real coming to grips with the revolution in ideas and feeling that is part of the computer age. The radical Jewish Left has pioneered the communal *havurah*. But the religious structure is irrelevant to the lifestyle of the average middle-class Jew, and even the most ambitious of avant-garde Jewish activity is burdened by nostalgia. There is so much fear among the rabbinic leaders that we will lose contact with our past that little energy survives to establish some kind of meaningful contact with the future. The burden of proof is distributed irrationally. Those who wish to make changes bear the most of it, even though what they resist has long since been ignored. Jews today often prove their right to their identity, not by doing what they need not defend, but by defending what they do not need.

Many are turned off by the parochialism of the Jewish community. In a mobile age when national boundaries are becoming less relevant and when the worlds of business and education demand social intermingling, the hysterical response of rabbinic leaders to intermarriage is deeply reactionary. Charges against Jews of tribalism and clannishness have usually been dismissed as the rantings of antisemites. But many Jews experience these attitudes as the normal response of their family and friends. They find themselves surrounded by a fear of openness and a passion for social isolation that belies the propaganda of liberalism which Jews associate with their image. An obsession with the question of Jewish survival dominates the work of the community and claims all energies. Jewishness becomes the ultimate criterion by which all activities are judged and by which all goals are evaluated. The result is stifling.

Many are alienated by the appeal to antisemitism. They are resentful of an establishment that seeks to frighten them into being Jewish. Group paranoia hardly seems an acceptable base for an affirmative identity. While one may have to be Jewish for negative reasons, he does not have to build an organizational identity out of a social disease. Moreover, young Jews do not perceive the American Jewish community as a destitute, downtrodden community. Having been raised in the affluence of middle-class suburbia and having tasted every opportunity for bourgeois success, they see their people as one of the wealthiest and most influential components of the American establishment. They perceive that the intellectual and financial resources of the Jewish world are too vast for only self-pity and self-defense, and that, with proper motivation and direction, they could be used for more humanistic ends. The self-image of the Jew raised in Hitler's era is different from the vision of his post-war child.

Many Jews are estranged by the vicariousness of contemporary Jewish experience. They recognize the obvious truth that the only Jewish reality that excites the majority of American Jewry is the state of Israel. In present day synagogues and community centers the programs for both youth and adults are overwhelmingly devoted to the culture and political problems of the Israeli people. While they do not deny the uniqueness and grandeur of the lifestyle in the Jewish state, and while they are eager to work for the survival of this nation, they find the Israeli experience a second-hand adventure. For those Jews who choose to be truly Zionistic and choose to emigrate to the Jewish homeland, Jewishness built around the excitement of Israeli patriotism is direct and authentic. But for the vast majority of American Jews it is an exercise in futility. By labelling Diaspora living as inferior, Zionism condemns the Jew who chooses to live in the Diaspora to be an "almost-Jew," to be a Jew who is incapable (by his place in the world) of being fully Jewish. The world of Jewish identity has been split in two. There are those who live Jewishness in the state of Israel, and there are those who stand on the sidelines and *kvell*. For a Jew who selects to be neither an Israeli nor a *kveller*, there are almost no options.

Many are driven away by the excessive nationalism that permeates the community leadership. Their education and their sentiments lead them to struggle for the humanist ideal of a unified mankind. Involvement in the affairs of the Jewish community only brings them problems of conscience. Instead of encountering the tradition of international culture, which Jews helped to pioneer in the nineteenth and twentieth centuries, they find themselves embroiled in the internal politics and foreign relations of a small Middle Eastern state, and discover that the United Nations and American disarmament are now the enemy. The concept of Jews as an international people, skeptical of all chauvinism, and committed by their history to world unity has become a soul without an institutional body to give it reality.

The alienation of so many American Jews from Jewish institutions and from any kind of positive Jewish association is deplorable. Not because being Jewish is important in and of itself, and not because Jewish survival has some religious or supernational significance which the rational person is unable to perceive, but because Jewish identity has a humanist and ethical value which mankind needs.

To be Jewish is to be a member of an international family whose structure and whose loyalty transcend the nationalist disaster of the contemporary world. The Jews are more than Judaism. They are more than Israel and the Zionist experience. They are more than a unique ethnic culture. They are, in experience, an 'internationality,' a people whose worldwide extension is a harbinger of future group identity in our rapidly changing world. For the past two centuries Jews have been the initiators and developers of cosmopolitan culture in the European environment. From Ludwig Zamenof to Albert Einstein, Jews have helped to pioneer the idea of a world society in which the primary social identity of each individual would be "human," and in which the ultimate group loyalty would be mankind.

If this humanistic ethic, strongly embedded in the modern experience of the Jewish people, can be divorced from the irrelevant supernatural trappings of the past, it will provide a secular Jewish alternative to both secular nationalism and to religious mysticism. A truly humanistic Judaism will create a Jewish alternative which is sorely needed and which has never been given an organized public expression.

A Jewish humanism, which is courageous enough to dispense with the hypocrisies of conventional religion, must be honest enough not to be all things to all people. It cannot with integrity satisfy the ethical and Jewish needs of every alienated Jew. If it tries to be meaningful to every Jew who is estranged from existing religious institutions, it will be meaningful to none. Some who are alienated want *more* religion, more supernatural experience, more mysticism. Others want *more* nationalism, more Zionism, more involvement with the state of Israel. To reject theology does not mean that one accepts humanism or humanistic ethics. Secular Jews can be as chauvinistic and parochial as religious Jews.

There is, in my mind, a personal and social need for an "ethical" institution which carries on the historic moral role of the conventional religious congregation, without the supernatural sanctions which a belief in God provided. Since there are many possible secular moral systems, there are many possible "ethical" congregations. A Humanistic Jewish temple is one that trains its members in a humanistic morality and in the humanistic value of Jewish identity.

The Jewish Personality

A non-Jewish friend confided to me certain feelings and observations that he was afraid to articulate in public. He revealed that during the past year he had been consumed by an irresistible desire to discover the source of Jewish intellectual distinctiveness and creativity. Fascinated by the liberal and antiauthoritarian character of most of the Jews he encountered in the academic and political world, he was intrigued by the origin of this phenomenon. In his intent to be a serious student he took the suggestion of every interfaith institute rabbi he encountered and proceeded to investigate the 'sacred' literature of the Jewish people. He spent many hours reading and rereading the Bible, patiently supplementing the classic with selected passages from the Talmud in English translation. Nevertheless, the more diligently he studied, the more puzzled he became. While he discovered many statements that were ethically significant and many stories that were aesthetically precious, he very quickly noted that the mood of the literature was conservative, pedantic rather than intellectual, and decidedly authoritarian. The Jew of the Bible and the Talmud seemed to have absolutely no relationship to the urbane, witty American Jew he so frequently encountered.

If I had been on my proper 'interfaith' toes I would have assured my friend that his reading of the ancient literature was superficial and without profound insight. I would have showered him with effusive compliments about the earthshaking influence of both the Bible and Talmud. I would have reminded him that the entire structure of contemporary Western religious civilization rests on the pronouncements of this sacred literature. I might even have tossed at him the observation that human moral sensitivity depends on the insights of the ancient Jewish writers. But I didn't have the heart—because he was *right*.

It is simply an observable fact, obvious to any reader who can transcend his interfaith defensiveness, that the 'ancient books' of Judaism do not correspond in mood and temperament to the reality of the modern Jew. While certain ethical continuity prevails, the chief characteristics that philosemites find so admirable in present day Jewry are totally absent. The distinguishing marks of internationalism, intellectuality, liberalism, humor, scepticism, and urbanity which earn the ecstatic praise of Jew lovers and the passionate denunciation of Jew haters are quite alien to the solemn and pious temperament of the writers. With the exception of the pseudosophistication of Ecclesiastes, temperamental identity between ancient past and modern present is essentially non-existent.

This reality points up the problem that the study of Jewish history presents. If, in our attempt to understand the nature of contemporary Jews and Judaism, we concentrate on the verbal utterances of famous authority figures, we shall achieve no more insight into the nature of the Jewish personality than my diligent Gentile friend. To concentrate our investigation on the famous or less than famous sayings of prophets and rabbis is to pursue the kind of naïve historical study that gives no indication of how we got from Jeremiah to Freud. It is to assume that the major forces influencing Jewish life arise out of the conscious instruction of official teachers, while the truth of the matter is quite the opposite. For the chief historical factors in Jewish development have been 'unconscious' and completely unarticulated by the prestigious figures of the past. We are what we are in many cases—not because of our sacred literature but in spite of it.

An honest Judaism is always more interested in the nature of the Jew than in the verbalizing of official

spokesmen. The problem with much of modern Jewish
education is an overemphasis on what Jews said they were
and an underemphasis on an objective and critical study of
Jewish history. Since religious institutions are notoriously
conservative, they are the last ones to reflect social change.
Their creeds and pronouncements often take many centuries to articulate the operating beliefs of a culture. To
explore the reality of what it means to be Jewish by tasting
the spoken words of famous ancient Jews is to taste each
cake by simply licking the frosting.

A few observations may clarify the thesis.

1. The overwhelming majority of modern Jews tend to be
internationalist in their outlook. While antisemitism and
the Hitler holocaust have made them passionate defenders
of Israel, and while social insecurity often turns the small-
town American Jew into a verbal superpatriot, fanatic
chauvinism is largely absent from the operating ideologies
of the Western Jew. Most Jews are identified with political
and social movements that subordinate nationalism to
international cooperation and view racial and cultural
differences as less significant than human unity. The
epithet 'the international Jew' with which the antisemite
assaults his enemy is, in reality, perceptive. Although the
bigot views internationalism as a sin, he rightly observes
that the contemporary Jew tends to regard national
boundaries as less significant than others.

To explain this phenomenon by picking odd quotations
from the Bible and Talmud is irresponsible. The sacred
scriptures exude a mood of passionate nationalism and
Zionistic fervor which back up the eternally sacred character of Palestine for the Jew with the firm endorsement of a
universal deity. Even the Messianic dream involves the
vindication of the superiority of Jewish insight and the
return of all Jews to their land. If it is true that Yahveh
punishes our people and complains about them, it is also
true that he has chosen us, and us alone, as his priests.

The internationalism of the Western Jew finds no congenial home in the old texts. It finds its source and

inspiration in the often unrecorded experiences of the Jewish dispersion. The Jew, the most passionate of ancient chauvinists, acquired the potential for universalism through the pain of his 'exile.' Dispersed to the four corners of the earth and regarded as an outlawed pariah by the Christian world, he became by necessity the first internationalist. Although his daily study introduced him to nationalistic fantasies, his daily experience divorced him from the intensity of local patriotism. To be a Jew required the mentality of the wanderer and the world citizen. His prayers may have been filled with devotion to Zion, but his realistic encounters made him wary of patriotic fervor. National chauvinism and antisemitism were too often companions. When the Emancipation came, the Jew had been transformed. Although he might verbally pose the superpatriot, his historical memories resisted the role. By his fears and not by his study he had been temperamentally converted.

2. The image of the modern Jew is that of the intellectual. Although the claim is a bit pretentious, it is certainly true that the European Jew, once exposed to the delights of university education, swallowed the experience more zealously than others. Jews today are noted for their penchant for secular education and the high value they place on the academician.

Yet nothing in their official literature would suggest such a bent. The Talmudic rabbis railed against the Greeks and denounced their style of inquiry. Neither the Bible nor the Talmud is structured in the logical way that would meet the minimum standards of a competent abstract thinker. Although literacy and Torah study were widespread among Jews, neither suggested intellectuality. For the character of the intellectual is not determined by the ability to read or by the amount of study. It is always determined by how one reads and studies. The curriculum of the Polish *heder* or *yeshiva* was no more intellectual than the study program of the Algiers Koran school.

The reputed verbal ability of the modern Jew is a much

better clue to the origin we seek. For intellectuality and abstract thinking always starts with a fascination with words. Verbal people enjoy words and the manipulation of words, and this disposition leads inevitably to logic and analysis. Skill with words is not the product of abstract thinking. The reverse is true; manipulating words is the mother of abstraction. If Jews are intellectual, it is because they became verbal.

The Jewish fascination with words is not the product of Bible study or prescription. If that were the case, the Muslims in their devotion to the Koran and the Protestants in their devotion to the Scriptures would be equally verbal. The Jewish attachment to words is the result of the indispensability of speech for Jewish survival. In the post-Talmudic period, when Jews were stripped of any form of physical defense and when they were thrust into the nascent professions of the middle class, the only weapon of survival the Jew possessed was the persuasion of speech. If words hold a special charisma for Jews, it is with good reason. By their power alone did Jews meet the assault of the outer world. The verbal finesse of the Polish Jew is not something the Talmud gave to the Jew; it is something the Polish Jew gave to the Talmud. When secular schools were opened to him, the European Jew brought the same precision to the social and physical sciences.

3. Jews, in the modern world, are notorious anti-authoritarians. They utilize a sceptical humor that deflates the pompous and shatters pretense; where others tend to be accepting of obedience, Jews resist it and find it emotionally necessary to question and challenge. Jewish creativity in the arts and sciences has largely been the result of Jewish willingness to resist conformity and defy established theories.

A free and healthy society requires a reasonable resistance to authority. And yet historic Judaism, no less than historic Christianity or Islam, was an authoritarian culture in which a scholar class posed itself as the guardians and interpreters of God's truth. While rabbis might disagree among each other, every rabbi in his own bailiwick, demanded obedience. And, while Jews might grumble and complain, they accepted the authority of the scholar class and did not resist. Within the community, the Jew was an obedient conformist and the temper of the Bible and Talmud re-enforced this attitude.

But the Jewish attitude toward authority was not determined after the dispersion so much by the inner community as by the outside world. Away from the comforts of 'home,' the Jew found himself placed in a general environment where the Gentile rulers were invariably hostile. The princes might talk a great deal about justice and mercy but the Jew was never the recipient of these ideals. As the centuries advanced, Jews developed a well-founded scepticism to outside authority. While within the framework of their own community, they remained loyally obedient; their attitude to the more powerful rulers that dominated their lives was one of severe reservation tinged with the revenge of laughter. When the trauma of the Emancipation destroyed the structure of the ghetto community, the free Jew then directed his long-acquired healthy scepticism to the authorities of the inner community. The rabbis and the sacred literature now received the critical grilling the Jew had repeatedly used against the commands of the Gentile world.

4. Jews today are generally regarded as liberals. Although the bigots of Wayne, New Jersey may find the quality reprehensible, philo-semites adore it. By the label 'liberal' we simply want to indicate that an individual finds social change desirable, as opposed to a 'conservative' who prefers to retain the status quo. The Jew of today is often a pioneer of change. If fashions alter, if new ideas are to be tested, the Jew is emotionally susceptible to try the new. Even in the promotion of social experiment, the Jew is conspicuous by his presence.

Why? Certainly, Jewish literary indoctrination is conservative. The sacred texts promote the immutability of the law and the eternity of the Torah. If changes are allowed, they are justified as painful necessities not as desirable events. When conservatives initiate change, they do so with sadness and reluctance. The mood of rabbinic Judaism is pervaded by this regret.

The contemporary Jewish mood owes little to this religious conservatism. If Jews are easily amenable to change, their adaptability is a function of their history not their official literature. Against their will, Jews were compelled by the necessities of persecution to adapt to new environments. Although their indoctrination denied the value of change, their experience affirmed it. Moreover, early in their dispersion Jews abandoned the agricultural and pastoral pursuits of their Biblical era and became reluctant devotees of city living. Urbanized as a people long before other groups, they abandoned the stable patterns of agrarian living for the more dynamic style of bourgeois existence. While their religious literature made heroes out of patriarchal shepherds with dispositions for simplicity and stability, the Jews assumed a new pattern of living within the city culture. It is a supreme irony that while the Jews have been among all European peoples the most addicted to urban living, the sacred literature that is supposed to define the Jewish personality is utterly divorced from it. Liberalism is a by-product of the most significant Jewish social experience—an experience which Sabbath study and Sabbath reading never reveal to any congregation.

The conclusion is clear. One will never discover the origin of the significant modern Jewish personality traits by studying the official texts of ancient times. Contrary to public belief, the Biblical and Talmudic periods are less significant in understanding the nature of the modern Jew than the almost unrecorded centuries of the Dispersion. The unconscious social forces that do not speak must be spoken for.

The Jews

When I was a teenager I found a copy of Hilaire Belloc's *The Jews*. The author's reputation for antisemitism had preceded him, and I was eager to discover his ideas on Jewish vice. Although the book was filled with fantasy and distortion, the image of the Jew, which the English man of letters possessed, was attractive. Belloc imagined that the Jew was incapable of national patriotism, and that his tribal loyalty made him part of an international people whom the present system of nation states could not comfortably abide. The Jew, the author reasoned, was more than a member of a distinct religious group, more than an example of ethnic loyalty. He was part of a unique, landless people who could no longer feel the blood and guts sentiments which motivated both peasants and aristocrats to die for their country.

Of course, Belloc lived before the establishment of the state of Israel, the trauma of the European holocaust, and the triumph of modern Zionism. He wrote at a time when the Jew was admired as a creator of cosmopolitan letters, hated as a manipulator of international finance, and feared as a leader of Bolshevik revolution. The Jewish obsession with the survival of a small Middle Eastern state was a situation of the future. The Rothschilds, Einstein, and Trotsky had not yet yielded to Ben Gurion and Golda Meir.

Belloc's feeling for the Jew was ambivalent. He found the international Jew both attractive and repulsive, and resolved his inner conflict through a patronizing anti-semitism. But his vision of the Jew had a nobility and grandeur that he never intended. Being no devotee of human unity and world government, he found Jewish activity to be subversive of that national exclusiveness which nationalism required, and denounced Jewish rationality and intellectuality as the products of rootlessness. What he disliked in the Jew as a political reactionary is precisely what the liberal humanist found most attractive.

The Jewish response to Belloc and his antisemitic contemporaries was shameful. Instead of affirming the cosmopolitan values which the Jewish vanguard had achieved, the apologists endorsed the value system of their accusers. For both the antisemite and his Jewish respondent national loyalty became a supreme value. If the apologist were a classical Reformer, he replied that the Jew was only Jewish because of his religion and that the Jew was as British, as German, or as American as his Christian neighbor. If the apologist were a Zionist, he replied that the Jew was in need of a national home where he could develop his own ethnic culture, and that once he was rooted in the land of Israel, he would display none of the abnormal symptoms of a gypsy people.

The histories of the Jewish people that are presently available reflect this defense. They are intended to prove that what the antisemite fears about the Jew is not real and that the Jew does not threaten the kind of world the antisemite wants to live in. The Jew can be as nationalistic and as patriotic as anybody else. The Jew can be as harmless and as innocuous as any other denomination. If the Jew is extraordinary, it is because of what he has inherited from the past, not because of what he has become in the present. In the world view of the apologist, the Jew is great because of what he has already given, not because of what he is about to give.

Current Jewish histories suffer many deficiencies. They spend too much time on religious experience. There is an overemphasis on the personalities of priests, prophets, and rabbis. There is an underemphasis on the vested interests that motivated their message. The authors of the Torah may have been sensitive visionaries in daily contact with Yahveh, but they certainly knew how to edit a document which maximized the political power of a hereditary priesthood. The sages of the Talmud may have been moral paragons, but they obviously promoted a doctrine of divine revelation which made the rabbi indispensable. In an America where Jews are trying to establish their identity as a religious group and where Bible heroes are their chief claim to fame in the Protestant hinterland, it may be politic to talk about the spiritual nature of Jewish experience. However, it is hardly accurate.

Popular historians devote too much energy to recording

the official beliefs of official teachers. There is a naïve assumption that Jewish behavior reflects the dogmatic utterances of theologians. There is a childish notion that Jewish people (or any people) act out what they say they believe. If true conviction is that set of ideas on which an individual is willing to act, then most people, including priests, prophets, and rabbis are unaware of what they truly believe. Too often the historian pays attention to the conscious testimony of testifiers without paying any attention to what they do. Too often the sociologist asks the Jew what he believes without observing how he behaves. If the researcher were to depend on what Jews say they believe to determine the character of the Jewish community, he would conclude that American Jewry is a collection of pious Torah lovers who never make any decision without consulting God. If he depends on how Jews behave, he would come to a contrary conclusion—that the overwhelming majority of American Jews find the Bible, the Talmud, prayer, and God completely irrelevant in the conduct of their daily business. Absence of introspection is the vice of all peoples. Jews are no exception.

Popular historians spend too much time on Bible history. The Torah and its supplementary books were written for a pastoral and agricultural society which the Jews graduated from over two thousand years ago. The urban culture which has determined the modern Jewish personality is unrelated to the experience of the authors of the sacred text. Jews who are embarrassed by their long connection with the city and its middle-class, and who regard farmers and shepherds as a more wholesome breed than "city-slickers" (and who, in particular like the early Zionists and Jewish socialists, find it degrading that Jews have lost contact with the soil and manual labor) revel in the Biblical period when Jews were normal peasants with a strong attachment to their native land. In Israel, the study of Jewish history places great emphasis on the glories of the Davidic period and the post-Herzl colonization of Palestine and skims over those intervening centuries when the Jews were a floating international people. The problem with such skimming is that it distorts the true nature of Jewish experience and fails to explain the Zionism it seeks to glorify. The Hebrew invaders of Joshua's day were desert nomads who were more primitive than the nation they conquered, while the Jewish colonizers of Balfour's time were the sophisticated intellectual products of an advanced urban culture. Between the two there is almost no analogy.

The conventional historian is much too obsessed with the persecution of the Jews. He senses the Jewish fear of antisemitism and the Jewish need to disarm their enemies. Pity and guilt have been the traditional Jewish defenses against pogroms. Stories of massacres and holocausts make the Jew a pitiable figure in the sight of potential haters and inhibit hostility. They also serve to re-enforce internal loyalty by increasing the anger of the Jew toward the Gentile world and by making him feel guilty about assimilation. Of course, no rational person can deny the fearful assaults on Jewish survival which are the standard fare of European history. But neither can any objective person deny that, throughout most of their history, the Jews have enjoyed long periods of prosperity and power. The Jews of Charlemagne's empire, of Omayyad Spain, of Khazar Scythia, and of Greek Alexandria are more typical of Jewish history than the victims of the Crusaders and Chmielnicki's legions. The Jewish personality was not molded by failure. It had its origin in the long centuries of urban success which were more characteristic of Jewish experience.

The popular writer often seeks to make the Jew unique in the wrong way. He seeks to prove that Judaism as an ideology is distinct and different from other religious ideologies. Since the religious aspect of Jewishness has always been the most respectable in the American environment, the writer is forced to find the special character of the Jew in an area where the Jew is least distinct. Christianity is singled out for invidious comparisons. It is denounced for vicarious atonement, puritanical sex, violence toward enemies, and a concentration on the afterlife, while Judaism is praised for having avoided these errors. How one discusses historic Judaism without reference to animal sacrifice, the seclusion of women, the Messianic punishment of the wicked, and the supernatural vision of the world-to-come, is as wondrous as the present Soviet rendition of the Bolshevik history without Trotsky and Stalin. If one is realistic, the theological uniqueness of official Judaism is negligible. In the end, authoritarian gods who demand exclusive worship behave pretty much the same way in any culture. They are manufacturers of useless guilt, imposing demands on human behavior that no one can satisfy. The real uniqueness of the Jew, which arises from his dispersion and his social role, often takes second place behind sterile ideological comparisons.

The conventional writer is often imprisoned by his own piety. He refuses to believe that the 'saints' of Jewish history were capable of mean motivations. While he applauds the humanness of David in lusting after Bathsheba, he resists the idea that David hired court historians to glorify his exploits and to denigrate the achievements of his arch-rival Saul—that the Biblical book of Samuel is nothing more than the edited propaganda of the ruling house. While he admits that Moses may have had a bad temper (praising the Torah for conceding this imperfection), he is appalled by the suggestion that the family of Moses created a biography of their dead leader and founder that bore no relationship to what actually happened and created the Torah to justify their authority. The struggle for power is a universal activity in all nations. Neither priests, nor prophets, nor rabbis were indifferent to its attraction. The institutions they created are testimonials to their ingenuity. The Jerusalem Temple is less interesting as an outlet for religious devotion and more interesting as a power device of a centralized priesthood. The Oral Law is less meaningful as an adaptation of the Torah law to the new conditions of urban living and more exciting as the ultimate justification for rabbinic authority. Traditional

Jewish leaders are often praised by community historians for having a positive attitude toward sex (unlike Christianity); they are less often cited for having a positive attitude toward personal power.

The popular historian is too frequently tempted to see the present in the past. He knows the insecurity of liberal Jews who seek to find authority for the changes they have made in the sanctions of ancient teachers. The leaders of the Reform movement, desperate to prove that their Judaism was as authentic and as venerable as orthodoxy, seized on the Biblical Prophets as the true founders of their religion. Blinded by their present need, they were unable to perceive that the desert morality of an Amos or an Elijah was more reactionary than the urban ethics of their conservative enemies, and that the authoritarian and self-righteous personalities of an Isaiah or an Ezekiel were more dogmatic than those of their rabbinic opponents. Under the doctoring of Reform historians, the Prophets emerged as social crusaders who would have found the French Revolution as congenial as a trip to Sinai. The result of this effort was a ludicrous connection. The Prophets were done an injustice by being portrayed as early-day Enlightenment reformers, and Liberal Judaism was badly served by being tied to an ancient argument that was no longer relevant. In many cases, the histories that emerge from "progressive" circles are less scientific than those emanating from traditional sources. The need to be "kosher" distorts the liberal vision.

VI
CONCLUSION

Objections

An excursion to a Catholic seminary provided an interesting opportunity for a discussion of the merits and demerits of modern humanism. The divinity students were eager to explore the consequences of a purely empirical approach to questions of truth. While they freely admitted the somewhat outmoded aspects of classical Thomist philosophy and the absurdities of traditional theology, they were equally sceptical about a consistently humanist approach to religious issues.

The reservations and objections of these perceptive students "boiled down" to three basic questions, and these three criticisms were voiced by four committed humanists who recently delivered their honest evaluation in a publication of the British Humanist Association. While the writers asserted that their intellectual training allowed them no philosophical alternative to an empirical ideology, they questioned whether the new thinking was as meaningful as the old doctrines it was replacing.

The three objections are these: (1) If humanism is a religion, then it must have some focus of worship. If that focus is no longer God, then it must be transferred to man;

and man, as he exists or can conceivably exist, is hardly worthy of adoration. In fact, the traditional humanist adulation of man and his possibilities is slightly amusing in view of his behavior. (2) The reality of the mystic experience cannot be denied. Millions of people in all cultures and religions have testified to it. To label it delusion or mental disturbance is glibly unsatisfactory, and to ignore it is to restrict the landscape of reality to what makes the scientific investigator comfortable. The transcendent and "supernatural" aspects of experience may be as factual as those occurrences that lend themselves to easy analysis. And (3) the meaningfulness of life arises out of the conviction that human goals are achievable, that what men fundamentally desire can be realized without eternal frustration. Traditional religion has always dealt with the obvious fact that no man ever transcends anxiety by promising blissful immortality on the individual level and Messianic salvation on the collective. But humanism, if it is empirical, must deny the significance of talk about the after-life or impetuous predictions about a "rosy future." Its realism deprives men of the old hope that sustains them.

It is obvious that if a religious humanism is to be viable, it must provide adequate replies to these objections. If it is to be a meaningful approach to the human condition, it must deal with the total religious experience and expectation. Let us therefore look at each of the criticisms.

1. Auguste Comte, the French founder of organized Humanism, inherited the optimistic mood of the eighteenth century rationalists. Universal education and economic reform were the keys to man's redemption. If effectively applied, they would transform the human beast into the adorable god. Man was capable of becoming what he already worshiped; therefore he was worthy of worship. He even went so far as to create a pantheon of humanist heroes who took the place of the old Jehovah and Christ. His proposals however, foundered on the rocks of two obvious realities. First, man proved in the industrial age to be considerably more beastly and considerably less adorable

than the formula suggested. While the new reforms socialized many, it reduced others to increased anxiety and
hostility. And secondly, to designate any portrait of man as
universally ideal and sacred is to imply that there is some
final end for which all men are intended and to deny the
apparent truth that ideals are a function of taste and
culture.

The second problem is really the more crucial. For the
classical notion of "sacredness" implies "taboo" untouchability; it suggests that what is holy or an object of worship
is beyond challenge, question, or probing. An idea or value
that is designated as sacred may be investigated, but it may
never be probed with the option of rejection. Adoration
inhibits analysis and understanding and prevents respect
from being intelligently conditional. The notion of sacredness is the historical foundation of idolatry, ancient and
modern. It takes words like "God," people like Marx, and
concepts like "the nation" and insulates them from sober
judgment and critical humor.

The secular age is founded on the principle of free inquiry
that shields no idea, value, or object from human probing.
Even the gods, if they were around would have to justify
their authority and subject themselves to psychological
testing. The classical concept of holiness and its attendant
response of worship are subversive of the entire mood of the
scientific age. To seek a religious substitute for God is a
foolish task; it is to compound one error with another. There
is no substitute, and there is no need of one. To worship
man is an absurdity. To respect individual men and ideas
while retaining one's sense of humor as an essential corrective is the only course of a pleasurable and meaningful
humanism.

2. Aristotle, the father of so much in modern philosophy,
unconsciously assumed that the structure of reality corresponded to the structure of the Greek language. His classification technique reflected the parts of speech in his native
tongue and projected the peculiarities of this versatile
speech into the universal scene. As a result, many of the

historic problems in philosophy are not "real" problems; they are the result of how the Greeks used their words to pinpoint differences and contrasts in the world they observed. Aristotle's philosophy was limited by his language.

Logic is, therefore, not something "out there," a reflection of the "real" order of the universe; it is the set of rules that underlies the use of a given language; and there are as many logics as there are distinct languages. Every rational system is therefore "inadequate," since there is no existent language capable of describing all distinctions in an infinitely complex world. Whole areas of human experience and observation cannot be handled by the tools presently available. In particular, in the area of feeling and emotion, English is hopelessly outmatched by the differences we observe but cannot describe. The word "love" has to do for "I love candy" and "I love my family."

No perceptive humanist denies the complexity of the universe or the arbitrariness of language. He does not assume that the reality he observes corresponds in some essential way to the words he uses or that it can be descriptively exhausted by the vocabulary he has at his disposal. He fully recognizes that there are many dimensions of experiences which we are still struggling to conceptualize and verbalize. In fact, it is precisely because he respects the integrity of these experiences that he prefers to avoid the misleading expressions of theological language.

The mystic experience is, most likely, authentic and real. It is undoubtedly possessed by a whole host of people who regard themselves as in no way "religious." A sense of oneness with the universe, accompanied by heightened feelings of tranquility and bodily transcendence, are universal and the private possession of no culture. No sensitive humanist would deny their meaningfulness nor seek to identify them with mental illness. His objection, if any, applies to the historic description. The traditional use of "God"-language to communicate the nature of this experience is the basic problem. The humanist emphatically denies that theological vocabulary (with all its unavoidable references to the personality of a deity) is the best available linguistic alternative to suggest the character of the religious "mystery." Instead of trying to force the mystic experience into a vocabulary mold that is better suited to the description of a celestial father-figure, the honest romantic should seek to enrich his native English by developing a more precise psychological language to communicate the quality of his ecstasy. The verbalizing mystic ought to use the best possible words he can put his tongue to. To do less is to prevent many people from seeing this experience as their very own.

3. For many traditional religions, including Judaism, Christianity, and Islam, happiness or salvation is some future event. Whether heaven, Paradise, or the Messianic age, it is a distant event that we work to achieve either by faith or deed. Every present, therefore, derives its significance from the future it anticipates; "today" is a means to "tomorrow."

Classical humanism of the nineteenth century gave up the mythology of the old religions but eagerly retained this messianic fervor. If only all men would dedicate themselves to the present conquest of poverty, disease, and ignorance, the blissful future of the ideal society would be ultimately achieved. The discipline of "now" was endurable because of the reward of "later." Disillusionment was the net result of this social analysis. No sooner was one set of problems solved, when another formidable set arose to take its place. No sooner did industrial civilization create prosperity and education, than the spectre of alienation and rootlessness emerged to haunt our urban culture. Every problem solved produced another; every desire satisfied spawned a dozen more.

If happiness is defined as a frustrationless state in the future, then it will never come; for every future turns out to be an anxiety ridden present. Even traditional concepts of heaven ruin eternal bliss with the pain of boredom, and drive the saints to dream of a new paradise. When eating is only a tool of survival, running a means of body development, and study a technique for improving the mind, then eating, running, and study have no intrinsic value but are captives of a future that replaces every solution with a new problem. Millions work and dream of retirement, and then retire and dream of work.

The clever humanist is never disturbed by the fact that all men die in the midst of problems. There is no "cure" for that condition, no matter how long a man lives; for that is what being alive means. Without the ability to perceive the intrinsic value of present things, immortality is an eternal agony of unfulfilled planning. Compassion does not derive its meaning from the harmonious social order it produces, but rather a harmonious social order is worth producing because it allows us to find the intrinsic pleasure of compassion. Intellectual discovery does not find its value in the increasing power it gives man to control his environment; controlling environment is worth pursuing because it enables man to taste the thrill of intellectual discovery. Men love to play games, not because they want to avoid problems, but because a game is the deliberate creation of a problem in order to enjoy the excitement of challenge. No man can understand mountain climbing by inspecting the top of the mountain.

Intelligent humanism never worries about the absence of a guaranteed "rosy future," since it is what we do in the present that gives meaning to tomorrow. Intrinsically valuable experiences are readily available "now." Whether we really achieve every goal we set out to pursue is really less significant than the pleasure of trying. If humanism merely perpetuates the traditional gloomy planning for the Messianic Age, whether earthly or heavenly, it will simply perpetuate the old anxieties under a new name. If it is to be genuinely insightful, it must learn to transcend the old promises with a sensitivity to fulfillment in the present.

Summary

In 1970, when the first meeting of the Society for Humanistic Judaism was held in Detroit, twelve principles were proposed as a statement of our shared philosophy. Much worthwhile discussion followed concerning the adequacy of the "manifesto." On the basis of this critique, I have revised the original twelve and reduced them to seven.

What follows is *my* view of the seven essential ideas of Humanistic Judaism.

Self-respect. The first question of any philosophy of life is: what is the goal of living? The traditional religious answer, whether Jewish or Christian, whether orthodox, conservative, or reform, is centered around the idea of God. For the traditional believer the purpose of human behavior is to find favor with God, to act in such a way that God finds him worthy of divine love and approval. The conventional liturgy of both Rosh Hashanah and Yom Kippur dramatizes this need for the feeling of heavenly endorsement. The ultimate divine punishment (especially in an age which has abandoned both paradise and hell) is divine disapproval.

The humanist denies the need for God's approval. He finds his goal of life in the experience of self-worth and self-esteem. Life is worthwhile when each man sees himself as worthwhile, when each man sees himself as significant and ultimately important. The humanist affirms that self-respect is distinct from both pleasure and happiness. Not all the activities that produce self-respect are pleasurable, and not all the procurers of short-run happiness achieve self-esteem. Happiness is not the goal of life but rather the consequence of having attained it. People who consciously pursue happiness rarely secure it; while people who consciously seek self-respect and acquire it, enjoy the long-run happiness we call fulfillment.

Humanism. Traditional religion has affirmed the weakness of man. It has denied that man can experience fulfillment without the guidance and assistance of God. It has denounced as an arrogant presumption that man is self-sufficient, that he possesses the power within himself to cope with all his problems and to control his future.

A humanist religion, on the contrary, affirms the power of

man. It finds no virtue in liturgies of human helplessness and dependence. It sees no merit in services of petitionary prayer. Theological faith in the saving power of God is diversionary; it prevents man from developing his own strength and experiencing his own competence.

Humanism glorifies the beauty and possibility of the human body and mind. A man capable of the self-discipline that yields self-respect is the ultimate work of art. Knowing that he himself has the power to solve his own problems and to satisfy his own desires gives him a sense of grandeur and nobility. Both the classic humanism of the Renaissance and the scientific humanism of the twentieth century share this ideal.

From the humanistic point of view, a good religion does not degrade man by emphasizing what he *cannot* do. It declares what man *can* do and elevates his self-esteem.

Autonomy. Self-respect is impossible without the experience of autonomy. The autonomous person feels that he is responsible for the basic direction of his life and that no one else has the right to usurp that responsibility.

Traditional religion denounced the concept of autonomy as blasphemous. It was certainly true that man was free to obey or to disobey God, but he obviously had no *right* to disobey. In the end, all theologists agree that man is subject to the authority of God, that God has revealed the behavior pattern that every man should follow, and that no man has the moral power to reject God's command. Like Job (and unlike Prometheus) the pious man continues to do what God asks him to do, even though his reason tells him that what God calls good is *really* bad. If the pious man rejects the authority of his priest or rabbi, he always does so in the name of God (like the protestant or reform Jew). He can only disagree about who speaks for God. He can never deny the right of God to command. In the end the theistic conservative and the theistic liberal accept authoritarian rule by an infallible king; and theology remains the mirror image of absolute monarchy or benevolent despotism.

For the humanistic Jew there is no authority, including

God, who must be blindly obeyed. Even if God exists, and even if his commands can be clearly determined, man has the moral right to challenge God's decrees. Whatever is not conducive to human self-respect is not worthy of human obedience, whether the source of its authority is the thunderbolt or the "still small voice."

Man does not derive his right to rule his own life from God. He derives it from his own evolved need for self-respect. Therefore, humanistic Jews are incapable of worship. Since there is no authority which is beyond human challenge, there is no authority which is sacred. The whole category of the sacred, with its overtones of taboo, untouchability, and unquestioning reverence, is incongruous with self-respect. The whole mood of worship is humiliating and degrading. Fawning praise of a supreme monarch has no redeeming virtue, even in the most splendid surroundings. The existence of God is irrelevent when the concept of God is morally objectionable.

The ideal man refuses to worship. But he does not refuse to respect and obey. Wherever any human authority, public or private, works to elevate the self-esteem of man, he will offer his conditional respect and obedience. The right to rule other men is a function of performance and wisdom. It is never eternal.

Community. Autonomy does not mean that each man is individually self-sufficient. It simply means that dependence is "horizontal" rather than "vertical." Other men, not God, are needed.

A humanistic view of life affirms the fact that man is a social animal, that every individual relies on the work and support of others, and that this dependence is expressed in the universal ability to love and to empathize. Individual man is nothing without his community. It is through contact with other men that he develops personality, and it is through cooperation with other men that he ensures survival.

Self-respect is possible only within the context of the human community. The power to be useful to others, the

power to help others, the power to give to others, is a source
of inner security and self-worth. The "selfish" man is
incapable of self-esteem. He is a frightened person who has
no confidence in his own power.

Humanists do not help one another and love one another
bacause they are commanded to do so by some higher
authority. They serve each other because their own dignity
depends on this action.

Rationality. Every philosophy of life must provide
some way for man to discover the truth about himself and
the universe in which he lives. Without this wisdom he will
never know how to help himself or to help others.

Traditional religion subscribes to what is called the
authoritarian approach to truth. In this procedure the truth
of a statement depends on who the *author* of the statement
is. For the orthodox Jew, it is sufficient to prove that "Moses
said it." For the Christian it is sufficient to prove that "Jesus
said it." For the Mohammedan you need go no further than
to demonstrate that "Mohammed said it." Even reform Jews
spend a great deal of time trying to prove that reform ethics
was authored by the Hebrew prophets.

The historic, religious truth game has always preferred to
test the truth of old statements by "name-dropping" and has
ignored the more relevant test of human experience. It has
always been more interested in finding out what some
famous authority figure of the past has had to say than in
checking the evidence of present living for new wisdom.

The humanistic Jew could "care less" whether Moses or
Hillel ever spoke. If what they had to say were true and valid,
their statements need not have their endorsement. They
can stand on their own worth.

A rational person is a man who is never impressed by
names. He simply wants to know whether there are any facts
to back up what people are telling him. Where there are no
facts available, he will be an agnostic, suspending judgment
until the evidence arrives.

For the humanistic Jew, no book, however famous, can
claim to be the eternal source of wisdom. The Torah, like any

book, must be tested by the procedures of scientific reasoning and common sense. In a world where useful information increases with each generation, it is more likely that Einstein and Darwin will have more to say to us about our place in the universe than will the Torah.

In the world of scientific reasoning, the wisdom of today may become the idiocy of tomorrow. There are no "eternal truths." Rational men live with temporary judgments and the possibility of surprise.

A humanistic Jew prefers science to faith in the Bible. He prefers Tchernikhovsky to the author of Job. He prefers Erich Fromm to Rabbi Akiva. He prefers new wisdom with supporting evidence to factless old beliefs in exotic packages.

The rational man is very emotional. He knows that love and empathy are essential to happiness. He knows that openness and laughter are essential to sanity. If he cultivates self-respect, he knows that self-respect is not an idea; it is a feeling, a strong feeling.

There are of course many emotions he seeks to avoid. Hate, envy, and self-pity are less than desirable. And so is a senseless worship of old books and dead men.

Religion. Traditional religion sees religion as the worship and service of God. Ethical rules are religious rules because God has commanded them. Nature festivals are religious festivals because the deity has ordered them. From the traditional point of view, since religion and theology are inseparable, Humanistic Judaism can be no religion.

However, the traditional assumption is false. Religion, as a practical activity, is usually independent of theological belief. Most Jewish people who call themselves religious have very vague and nebulous theological notions, if any. What they share with each other is *not* a strong belief in God but *rather* a strong attachment to certain ritual practices. The majority of these practices are associated with two calendars: the seasonal calendar of Rosh Hashanah, Sukkot, Hanukkah, and Passover, and the life-cycle calendar of baby-naming, Barmitsvah, marriage, and death. Both calendars together define the nature of Jewish religious behavior.

Each of these calendars can be given either a supernatural meaning or a natural meaning. Passover originated in ancient Palestine as a festival of spring. In later years it was attached to a miraculous story about how God saved the Jews from Egyptian slavery. As a festival of spring the holiday is no less meaningful than as a festival of Yahveh.

The calendar of the seasons and the calendar of human development are intimately related. They are both expressions of the rhythms of life on our planet. They are both celebrations of life.

Religion, as a practical activity, is man's way of identifying with the life process out of which he emerged. It is the way he dramatizes his connection with animate nature. Jewish religious activity did not begin with a belief in God; Jewish religious activity began with a festival of fertility and a festival of rain and a festival of light. Theology was a way wise men in the past sought to explain the purpose of these holidays long after the original purpose had been forgotten.

A humanistic Jew finds meaning in the celebration of life. He does not see himself as part of some isolated species dropped from heaven, and inferior to its creator. He sees himself as the supreme fulfillment of the evolutionary process, whereby life has become conscious of itself. With man the evolutionary process ends and the creative process begins. From now on, whether he likes it or not, man has the power to determine the nature of the life forms to follow. He has the power to design his own children. He has the power to fashion his own posterity. Unconscious evolution has yielded to conscious creation. Unlike the old story where the gods come first and life comes after, the scientific story reverses the religious order. First comes life, and then arises the possibility of the gods.

Judaism. There are three kinds of Jews who are

neither honestly orthodox, conservative, or reform. They are the involuntary, the ethnic, and the humanistic.

The involuntary Jew is the individual of Jewish descent who finds no meaning either in his past or in the unique practices of his ancestral religion. He fears antisemitism and feels guilty about departing the fold so long as there is any danger to the group. His Jewish affiliation is negative. His enemies are responsible for what he is. And he does not have the power to resist their definition.

The ethnic Jew is the person of Jewish descent who bears a strong attachment to the Hebrew and Yiddish cultures out of which he emerged. Both humanism and religion are secondary to his primary goal of rescuing Jewish national identity. His very intense feeling for Israel is not merely the fear of another holocaust; it is a positive and profound love for his national homeland. If he has the strength to act out his conviction, he moves to Israel, since only in Israel can he truly live as an ethnic Jew.

The humanistic Jew is an individual, of either Jewish or non-Jewish descent, who believes in the ultimate value of self-respect and in the principles of humanism, community, autonomy, and rationality. He also finds meaning in the celebration of life as expressed through the historic Jewish calendar and seeks to interpret this calendar in a naturalistic way. He perceives that the power he possesses to determine and control his own life is the result of two billion years of evolutionary history. Therefore, his religious feeling re-enforces his sense of human dignity.

A humanistic Jew, because of a common history and shared religious practices, feels a strong bond to Jews throughout the world. He also feels an important tie with all men who seek to promote individual self-esteem.

GLOSSARY

BEEMA — The reader's platform in the synagogue.

BOBE — Yiddish for 'grandmother.'

HALAKHA — The way. The lifestyle of the traditional Jew as described by the authorities of the Talmud.

HAVARAH — A small Commune.

HEDER — A one-room Hebrew elementary school.

HUTSPA — Gall.

HUTSPADIK — Full of *hutspa*. Full of gall.

KVELL — Yiddish for 'to take pride in.'

MISHPAKHA — Family.

PILPUL — The special methods of interpretation which Polish rabbinic scholars applied to Biblical and Talmudic texts.

SCHMALTZ — Yiddish for 'fat.'

SHTETL — Yiddish for 'town.'

YESHIVA — An academy of Talmudic study presently used for the training of rabbis.

ZAYDE — Yiddish for 'grandfather.'